DREAM TRACKS

THE RAILROAD AND THE AMERICAN INDIAN 1890–1930

NO. 107

Raton Tunnel N.M.
on A.T. & S.F. R.R.

Riddle
Photo

DREAM TRACKS

THE RAILROAD AND THE AMERICAN INDIAN 1890–1930

BY T.C. MCLUHAN

WITH PHOTOGRAPHS FROM THE WILLIAM E. KOPPLIN COLLECTION

HARRY N. ABRAMS, INC., PUBLISHERS, NEW YORK

IN THE DUST WHERE WE HAVE BURIED THE SILENT RACES AND THEIR
ABOMINATIONS WE HAVE BURIED SO MUCH OF THE DELICATE MAGIC
OF LIFE.

D.H. LAWRENCE[1]

I DO NOT ADDRESS MYSELF TO NATIONS BUT ONLY TO THOSE FEW PEOPLE
AMONGST WHOM IT IS TAKEN FOR GRANTED THAT OUR CIVILISATION . . . DOES
NOT DROP FROM HEAVEN BUT IS, IN THE END, PRODUCED BY INDIVIDUALS.
IF THE GREAT CAUSE FAILS IT IS BECAUSE THE INDIVIDUALS FAIL, BECAUSE I
FAIL. SO I MUST FIRST PUT MYSELF RIGHT. AND AS AUTHORITY HAS LOST ITS
SPELL I NEED FOR THIS PURPOSE KNOWLEDGE AND EXPERIENCE OF THE
MOST INTIMATE AND INTRINSIC FOUNDATIONS OF MY SUBJECTIVE BEING SO
AS TO BUILD MY BASE UPON THE ETERNAL FACTORS OF THE HUMAN SOUL.

C.G. JUNG[2]

IN THE UNITED STATES THERE IS MORE SPACE WHERE NOBODY IS THAN
WHERE ANYBODY IS. THAT IS WHAT MAKES AMERICA WHAT IT IS.

GERTRUDE STEIN[3]

THE MEANING OF AMERICA IS SIMPLY THAT ITS MEANING
CANNOT BE FIXED.

PERRY MILLER, AMERICAN SCHOLAR AND HISTORIAN[4]

ACKNOWLEDGMENTS

To Dave Fawcett, I owe many enlightening conversations on native culture and society. I am particularly indebted to him for his numerous and thoughtful suggestions throughout the writing of the book.

To Dr. Herb Terrace I am especially grateful for his assistance in the learning of a new craft: the art of computer technology! My many thanks to him for the use of his computer terminal at Columbia University in the preparation of my manuscript and for his many helpful comments throughout the final stages of its completion.

I am indebted to Dr. Robert Murphy for inviting me to Columbia University as a Visiting Scholar in anthropology. This allowed me to utilize the immense research resources of the university and contributed to a much richer manuscript.

I thank Anne-Marie Perier, Didier Guerin, and Nicolas Hugnet in Paris, France, for their persevering belief in the book. I also thank Sonny and Bert Lee for their unfailing belief in the project, for their concern that it come to fruition, and for their willingness to help out at all times.

My thanks to Dick Rudisill, Curator of Photographic History at the Museum of New Mexico, for his invaluable assistance in my research endeavors while I was in Santa Fe; to Jim Nottage at the Kansas State Historical Society for his many helpful suggestions; to Don Humphrey for aiding me in the identification of materials.

I would also like to extend my thanks to Paul Benisek and Susan Saltzer at Santa Fe Industries, Inc., Chicago, for their generous assistance in the tracking down of pictures and in providing me with copies for publication. I am particularly grateful to Mr. Benisek for allowing me to quote from the Atchison, Topeka and Santa Fe correspondence files. To W. E. Flohrschutz and Mike Martin at the ATSF offices in Los Angeles, I express my gratitude for their aid in my research and for making it possible for me to photograph and reproduce many of the early Santa Fe posters and brochure materials.

And my thanks to my friends who were there—for their patience, understanding, and good-naturedness during the research and writing of the book.

Above and at right: The California Limited at Laguna Pueblo, New Mexico, 1920s

Page 2: Raton Tunnel, New Mexico, c. 1885

Page 3: On November 14, 1926, *The Chief* departed Los Angeles with the stars of M-G-M's *War Paint* on board. Hollywood actors, these Indians helped the Santa Fe promote the occasion and also lobbied for better pay in their professional work.

The William E. Kopplin Collection

The author wishes to extend her gratitude to the Kopplin family, Bill, Hester, and Dorothy, and to Kopplin & Lee Images, for their cooperation and assistance in making the lantern images available for publication. The lantern slides were part of the estate of the late William E. Kopplin, who worked for more than twenty years in the advertising department of the Atchison, Topeka and Santa Fe Railway.

Designers: Nicolas Hugnet, Bob McKee

Library of Congress Cataloging in Publication Data
McLuhan, T. C. (Teri C.)
  Dream tracks.
  Includes index.
  1. Indians of North America—Southwest, New—Pictorial works. 2. Advertising—Southwest, New—Railroad travel. I. Title.
E78.S7M38   1985   979'.00497   85–6148
ISBN 0–8109–0835–2

CONTENTS

Taos Pueblo, New Mexico. San Geronimo Fiesta, relay race 1902

INTRODUCTION

"Then one by one they retired to their homes and we began to realize that we were still in America. One becomes so interested, so anxious to see it all, that he almost forgets, and it seems like a dream."[1]

These words—noted in the diary of a well-known traveler and photographer upon his first witnessing a Pueblo Indian ceremonial in 1897—reveal the hope of discovering connections with native origins, about which so little was known. Travel for this individual and for many other Americans, particularly travel to the exotic West, promised endless epiphanies for future memories. Countless new horizons still existed, and the air was full of expectation.

The increased mechanization of life at the turn of the century led to a conspicuous absence of the traditional and the spiritual—a lack of completeness. A growing interest in patterns of life other than our own took root and came to have validity and significance. The American Indian emerged from a position of banishment to a fanciful, factual, and appealing place in the pantheon of the American imagination.

Native culture held the earth as sacred and inviolate—not to be torn up, but to be lived in, in a state of grace and harmony with the beneficent power emanating from the rhythms of nature—a power for living that the modern world had forgotten. "They had what the world lost," wrote John Collier of the American Indian. "They have it now. What the world has lost, the world must have again, lest it die. Not many years are left to have or have not, to recapture the lost ingredient."[2]

Most of the pictures in this book are deceptively familiar. They represent a world of social myths that speak a language we know, have grown up with, and even dreamed about. For these reasons, and because of their widespread popularity, I have chosen to present these images as a single canvas in the realm of rhetoric and patriotism. Anthropologist C. B. Lewis has pointed out that "the

Tewa Indians of Santa Clara Pueblo perform the Eagle Dance for the Fred Harvey/Santa Fe "detourists"
who were bused into the pueblo for the event, 1927

folk has neither part nor lot in the making of folklore." This observation seems to be particularly apt in the case of the corporate image-making machinery of the Santa Fe Railway and its novel presentation of "primitive" life and the wilderness. The image makers, through their photography, painting, and illustration, contributed significantly to the "Americanization" of the Indian. What has emerged is a fascinating alchemy of "history," native life, and the great American West.

To explore the dynamic patterns of image making by one of America's most powerful institutions—the railroad—is to enter a world of both illusion and reality. That many of the myths fostered by the railroad have come into conflict with reality is no surprise. I have not attempted in any way to adjudicate the contradictions that were an inherent part of the thinking of the era but, rather, to arrest them for contemplation.

The captions for the pictures are an attempt to move beyond the dream of culture that the Santa Fe advertising department so successfully constructed. They are an endeavor to touch the intangible realms of memory, dream, hallucination, and meditation, whose very centers are mirrored deep in all aspects of native American life.

The William E. Kopplin collection, which comprises the lantern-slide illustrations in this book, is presented for the first time. It is a remarkable body of delicate and luminous images taken between 1890 and 1930—all of them hand-colored glass plates—brief glimpses of another culture, which do not necessarily link image with society. Nonetheless, what they have come to mean is what makes them worthy of study and appreciation. These images of Indian life and the wilderness imbued the public with popular notions about Indians and the American Southwest landscape. Through the railroad, they became a major vehicle in the quest for roots and a sense of belonging, at a time when man was experiencing "uncertainty in the strivings of the soul."

THERE ARE EPOCHS . . . WHEN MANKIND, NOT CONTENT WITH THE PRESENT, LONGING FOR TIME'S DEEPER LAYERS, LIKE THE PLOWMAN, THIRSTS FOR THE VIRGIN SOIL OF TIME.

OSIP MANDELSTAM [3]

"FATHER, REMEMBER, WE'RE LIVING IN THE TWENTIETH CENTURY!"
"THE TWENTIETH CENTURY! I COULD PICK A CENTURY BLINDFOLDED OUT OF A HAT AND GET A BETTER ONE!"

DIALOGUE FROM BILLY WILDER'S FILM *SABRINA* [4]

CORPORATE IMAGE MAKING AND PRIMITIVE CULTURE

RAILWAY CULTURE: A CALL TO A NEW PATRIOTISM

To the men who run the railways of the country, whether they be managers or operative employees, let me say that the railways are the arteries of the nation's life and that upon them rests the immense responsibility of seeing to it that these arteries suffer no obstruction of any kind, no inefficiency or slackened power.

President Woodrow Wilson (1917)[1]*

The modern world cracked down on the dawn of the new century with implacable force. Society was in ferment. It was a time when machinery was hymned. Factories and industries, steadily expanding, yielded more goods for more people than ever before. But with the dramatic advances in technology and new sources of great wealth came great social dislocation. The passionate acceleration of growth and profit flung its vague tonnage like wind, disrupting lifeways and creating unprecedented ruptures that threatened the environment. Strange new rhythms, powerful enough "to blast a man's brain to imbecility by the surprise of it," inhibited human engagement.[2] The velocity of modern life produced by the new technologies was alienating. A wintry world of mechanical routine dwarfed the human aspect.

It was also a time of vast exaltation and exhilaration, of unbridled competition and unregulated speculation. A great new society was being formed, and with it came unheard-of frontiers of opportunity and ingenuity. The acceleration of time and the telescoping of distance added novel dimensions to the human condition. These changes were given their greatest impetus by the railroad. The locomotive bore into the wilderness like a wild eagle, arcing, speeding, breaking open virgin territory, fuming beatifically through the trampled lilies, humming the age mechanical.

During the early nineteenth century in America, the locomotive had become a national obsession, though there were differing views of its value. ". . . snort! puff! scream!—here he comes straight-bent through these feral woods, like the Asiatic cholera cantering on a camel . . ." harangued

Bibliographic sources and commentary are provided in detail in Notes and References, pp. 192ff.

AMERICAN PROGRESS, A CHROMOLITHOGRAPH AFTER A JOHN GAST PAINTING OF 1872, ISSUED IN GEORGE CROFUTT'S WESTERN WORLD, *1873*

The artist, according to the description on the back of the picture, illustrates "at a glance the grand drama of Progress in the civilization, settlement and history of our own happy land." In showing the progress of civilization according to nineteenth-century evolutionary assumptions, the artist has the Indians, along with bears, wild horses, and buffalo, fleeing before the Spirit of Progress, who wears the star of empire on her forehead, carries a book representing common school education, and trails a telegraph wire behind her. Following her are the various stages of transportation and the different occupations to trace the growth of civilization and the westward movement of American society.[3]

Herman Melville, who did not see "that iron fiend" as a great improvement of the age.[4] For Walt Whitman there was no greater wonder than the railroad. Commenting on "the distances joined like magic" and recounting his experience as a traveler, he wrote, "What a fierce wild pleasure to lie in my berth at night in the luxurious palace-car, drawn by the mighty Baldwin—embodying, and filling me, too, full of the swiftest motion, and most resistless strength! . . . The element of danger adds zest to it all. On we go, rumbling and flashing. . . . "[5] Emily Dickinson enjoyed the sight of an approaching train:

> I like to see it lap the miles
> and lick the valleys up . . .[6]

while Emerson has confided to us his "dreamlike travelling on the railroad."[7] Hawthorne, on the other hand, protested "the long shriek" of the locomotive, "harsh, above all other harshness," telling a story "of all unquietness."[8] Hart Crane reacted skeptically to the new railway technology, describing it as an "empire wilderness of freight and rails."[9]

Another example of the rhetoric of technology, as it relates to the locomotive, is illustrated by Thomas Wolfe's reflections of pride and hope in train travel: "In America, the train gives one a feeling of wild and lonely joy, a sense of the savage, unfenced, and illimitable wilderness of the country through which the train is rushing, a wordless and unutterable hope as one thinks of the enchanted city toward which he is speeding, the unknown and fabulous promise of the life he is to find there."[10]

In Europe, we encounter a similar scene. Wordsworth loathed this "profane innovation." For Charles Dickens, the Iron Horse had the effect of "an earthquake, accompanied with thunder and lightning," releasing "unknown languages in the air, conspiring. . . ."[11]

Verlaine was entranced by the hurtling rhythms of the railroad train, likening the new panoramic experience to a novel melody:

> The scene behind the carriage window-panes
> Goes flitting past in furious flight; whole plains
> With streams and harvest-fields and trees and blue
> Are swallowed by the whirlpool, whereinto
> The Telegraph's slim pillars topple o'er
> Whose wires look strangely like a music-score.[12]

In a letter dated August 22, 1837, Victor Hugo lamented the distortions of the countryside he experienced from a speeding train window: "The flowers by the side of the road are no longer flowers but flecks, or rather streaks, of red or white; there are no longer any points, everything becomes a streak; the grainfields are great shocks of yellow hair; fields of alfalfa, long green tresses; the towns, the steeples, and the trees perform a crazy mingling dance on the horizon; from time to time, a shadow, a shape, a spectre appears and disappears with lightning speed behind the window: it's a railway guard."[13]

Ironically, there emerged, from the disparate reactions stimulated by the new railway culture, a rhetoric of technology—one that contrasted sharply with the prevailing tradition that glorified the sanctity of the wilderness. That attitude gave rise to a rhetoric of nature. By the turn of the century, the Atchison, Topeka and Santa Fe Railway, through a dazzling diversity of advertising themes, established what needs to be recognized as a *rhetoric of belonging*—one that made assertions about soil, roots, and country. The effect was to reduce the inevitable estrangement between man and nature that began with the birth of the railroad. The photographs, lantern slides, illustrations, and calendar art of Indian life in the American Southwest that appear in this book represent different facets of all three rhetorics. In that sense, these visual arts were the basic ingredients of a novel amalgam in the history of American business: that of corporate image-making and "primitive culture."

The Atchison, Topeka and Santa Fe Railway Corporation would "discover" the powerful and poetic uses of the wilderness and Indian life and market them to establish for the railroad a rich national identity. The growth of business for the Atchison, Topeka and Santa Fe became as important to it as the development of a strategy to link the desert Southwest and its veiled kingdoms of unknown cultures to the railroad's extensive transportation system and the unique services it offered along its routes.

New and persuasive images of the Southwest territory and the life that inhabited the region were needed to dispel the public's apprehension of traveling through a seemingly forbidding terrain of desert and mountain. As the frontier receded historically and geographically, it loomed larger and larger imaginatively. This state of affairs provided the advertising department of the Atchison, Topeka and Santa Fe with a unique opportunity to create a fascinating new world of image-making freighted with the scent of earth and with evocative aspects of Native American life.

TOURISTS POSING AT TRADING POST WITH NAVAJO WOMAN AND INDIAN MAN

WILDERNESS AND THE AMERICAN SPIRIT

. . . In Wildness is the preservation of the World. Every tree sends its fibres forth in search of the Wild. . . . From the forest and wilderness come the tonics and barks which embrace mankind.

Henry David Thoreau (1863)[1]

. . . the gorgeous interior scenery of some of our western and southern districts . . . [is] a realization of the wildest dreams of paradise. . . . In fact, the real Edens of the land lie far away from the track of our most deliberate tourists . . . no fiction has approached it . . . and *beauty* is indeed, its sole character.

Edgar Allan Poe (1844)[2]

At the same time that the railroad began to dominate the American landscape, an unprecedented awareness of the natural wonders of the land took root. As W. B. Yeats has observed, new experiences elicit an "emotion of multitude."[3] Consider one traveler's recollection of his first visit to the Grand Canyon, one of nature's wildest beauties: "People . . . looked on speechless until they fainted or prayed . . . [and] some . . . simply marvelled at the scene or complained of the cost."[4] Upon first viewing the Catskill Mountains, Washington Irving wrote in 1851 about "the most witching effect"[5] the scenery had on his imagination. The spectacle of Niagara Falls provoked a traveler to feel "thunderstruck at the grandeur and magnificence of such an awful sight."[6]

Until the first third of the last century, America was caught in the rhythms of her own wildness, in the untamed thunder of her own deep. Wildness was her most distinctive feature. The country was to know no greater Eden, for it would soon be tamed into a garden hushed.

By the close of the century, the machine was in the garden, having overtaken sacred mountains, awesome waterfalls, epic plains, and primeval forests.[7] The course was unalterable. Free enterprise had little sympathy with the picturesque, and the railroad was no exception. With each new technological development came the relentless destruction of "landscapes." "It was all prices to them," wrote the poet and astute observer of American history, Archibald MacLeish; "they never looked at it: why should they look at the land? they were Empire Builders: it was all in the bid and the asked and the ink on their books."[8] Moreover, any restraint upon enterprise was considered un-American and "the man who could get his hands on the biggest slice of natural resources was the best citizen. Wealth and virtue were supposed to trot in double harness."[9]

The prevailing climate of ideas produced the fallacious assumption that the country's resources were inexhaustible. Progress was deified. As a goddess, she appeared as an angel carrying with her a book of knowledge and the weapons of the new technology, the telegraph and the railroad.[10] That "benevolent genie" lost no time in penetrating deeply and irrevocably into the fabric and texture of the indigenous life of the American wilderness. The railroad was to discover culture in the wilderness and, recognizing its potential, took up at once the task of exploiting it.

As the twentieth century was saluted with the new canons of technology, America was on the advancing edge. It was a time of spontaneity. The here and the now. The wonder of it all. The frontier was rapidly disappearing under foot, and land was quickly becoming real estate. American Indians were forced to abandon their homes, dismantle the center of their world, and move into a disoriented world of fragments—in the words of poet Robert Lowell, into "a wilderness of lost connections."[11] They were cut off from their land, the umbilical cord to their souls, and buried under the speculation and greed of Western expansion. The swift and increasing appropriation of land was of great concern to the Indian. An old Wintu woman of California was moved to ask: "How can the spirit of the earth like the White man? . . . Everywhere the White man has touched it, it is sore."[12]

An aggressive new world was taking shape. The rush of immigration westward continued, but America, dominated more and more by the proliferation of new and uprooting technologies, found its identity elusive. The new urban crowds were unaccustomed to the exploding wilderness of noise and grinding labor that characterized the new cities. There was an uneasiness that perhaps the "picturesque" had outlived its meaning and its usefulness. Spiritual impoverishment sent many in search of new meccas, and America turned inward, seeking guidance through mythology and legend. These would prove to be powerful tools, capable of establishing a sense of place, of belonging, of identity. A quest for "an enlightening of the spirit" became a quest for unity.[13]

From the scarred shadows of American grandiosity and expansion into new territories, emerged the image makers of the Santa Fe Railway. In an outpouring of patriotic spirit and image-building, they appealed to nationalistic pride to "re-capture the first fine careless rapture"[14] in a journey of discovery. A call to get to know one's country was spread throughout the land. Through the advertising mechanisms of the Atchison, Topeka and Santa Fe Railway, the nation gained much of its awareness of American Indian life and the wilderness.

THE SANTA FE RAILWAY: THE EMERGENCE OF THE NEW IMAGE MAKERS

Railroad iron is a magician's rod, in its power to evoke the sleeping energies of land and water.
Ralph Waldo Emerson (1844)[1]

At the beginning of this century, the Santa Fe Railway was engaged in a fierce struggle with other railroads for its share of the tourist and freight traffic in the American Southwest. The origins of the railroad were, however, quite humble. In 1859, the Atchison & Topeka existed only on paper as a railroad chartered by the Kansas State Legislature. The name Santa Fe was added four years later, in 1863, in the hope of securing financial support from the federal and state governments. Shortly afterward, the Atchison, Topeka and Santa Fe came to be known simply as "The Santa Fe."[2]

It was not until 1869 that the first tracks were laid. They ran a mere twenty-seven miles from Topeka to Burlingame, Kansas. One year and thirty-four miles later, the railroad had extended itself to Emporia, Kansas. Its first dramatic growth, however, resulted from its frantic effort to extend some 380 miles westward to the Colorado border. By reaching that goal in 1873, the Santa Fe Railway satisfied the terms of a federal land grant and took title to three million acres of land situated in western Kansas along the Arkansas River. The Santa Fe soon sold every acre of this land to settlers, thereby creating a strong financial base for further expansion that would bring it into direct competition with other railroads—the Kansas Pacific, the Southern Pacific, and the Denver and Rio Grande—for territory in the Southwest. The next two decades witnessed some of the most cutthroat efforts to dominate access from Colorado to California through what would later become the states of New Mexico and Arizona.

One remarkable episode of this struggle merits specific mention. In a unique incident in railroad-building history (1877–78), two hostile railroad corporations—the Santa Fe and the Denver and Rio Grande—felt compelled to maintain armed forces in the field to protect their territorial claims. That they took this extreme measure was a reflection of the desperation that each side felt in their race to lay track through the strategic Raton Pass—the only available gateway from Colorado south to the high plains of New Mexico. By virtue of a few hours' head start, the Santa Fe Railway barely won that race.

More typical of the entrepreneurial conflicts of the 1870s and 1880s between the Santa Fe and its main rivals were price wars and invasions of competitors' territories through extensive branching of feeder lines from main routes. Indeed, the greatest period of railroad building in the United States was between 1880 and 1890, when seventy thousand miles of new track were built. Although there was a great deal of building after 1890, most of America's leading lines were built before that time.[3]

Initially, the Santa Fe's branching strategy led to the demise of at least one of its competitors, the Kansas Pacific. Steady expansion, however, was not without its risks. The construction of a major new route from Kansas City to Chicago did not generate sufficient revenue to offset the high cost of building that route. This problem was compounded by an overly liberal dividend policy. Instead of reinvesting its earnings to cover maintenance and construction costs, the Santa Fe sought to satisfy its stockholders. By 1893, the Santa Fe's unrelieved greed for new territory and its unsound financial policies led to its bankruptcy.

In 1896, just as the railroad had struggled out of receivership, the new president of the Santa Fe, E. P. Ripley, was faced with the immediate problems of removing the stigma of recent bankruptcy and the railroad's callous image as an arrogant practitioner of nineteenth-century free enterprise. What was needed were new and essential sources of respectability.

Ripley began to study seriously the possibilities of using advertising to enhance the image of that battered "streak of rust." Previously, Santa Fe advertising was an unexplored force that, at best, was practiced crudely. The Santa Fe began to devote itself to the heritage of America, the wilderness, and the Indians. With patriotic drama and allure, the railroad's advertising became a sustained hymn to *natural* America. The imagination was encouraged to roam into the farthest reaches of the wilderness, where an ideal new world was promised—the exotic and simple

GERALD CASSIDY, INDIAN DETOUR, c. 1922

The painting (oil on canvas, approximately 82½ × 135") is printed by courtesy of La Fonda Hotel, Santa Fe, New Mexico, where the original is on display. Reproduced here for the first time, it is a magnificent example of Gerald Cassidy's mural-sized illustrations of historic events. A sufferer from tuberculosis, Cassidy first settled in Albuquerque in 1912, and then moved to Santa Fe two years later. He was one of the pioneers of the Santa Fe artists' colony, also painting commercial Western scenes for railroad posters. He received recognition as a serious painter with a mural The Cliff Dwellers of the Southwest *and with his* San Juan. *(Photograph by Robert Nugent)*

life of an earthly paradise. But in the process, promotional genius had to overcome the sobering actuality of this last outpost, which has been referred to as "a land of low esteem, the most scorned portion of the Great American Desert, [where] rugged mesas and towering mountains separated arid plains on the east from parched deserts on the west. . . . By contemporary standards, the Southwest's heartland was a desperate region, its principal value to the nation a geographic connective tissue that accommodated several transcontinental railway lines linking the Mississippi Valley and the Pacific Coast."[4]

The desert plateaus of the Southwest were often the scene of stark confrontations with the more disagreeable aspects of nature, where moments of intensity dominated. Sudden electrical storms could flatten everything in sight, and without a moment's warning, flash floods would make

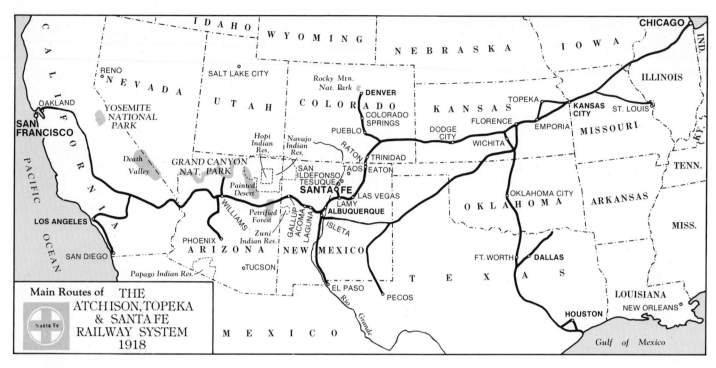

Map redrawn by Christopher L. Brest

passage impossible. In this land of dust storms and awful heat with its destroying, parching dryness, one crossed a thankless threshold of strangeness, vividly described by Mark Twain in a letter to his mother in 1861: "No flowers grow here, and no green thing gladdens the eye. The birds that fly over the land carry their provisions with them. . . . When crushed, sage brush emits an odor which isn't exactly magnolia and equally isn't exactly polecat—but is a sort of compromise between the two."[5]

But along the way there were scattered splendors, and the Santa Fe had the right-of-way through some of the most astonishing scenery in Creation. By emphasizing the latter, the railroad set about its task of mining the landscape for culture, the culture for artifacts, and the country for tourist traffic. Recognizing that the wilderness of the West offered aesthetic and spiritual values not attainable in the urban metropolis, it promoted tourism as the new religion.

It fell upon the shoulders of William Haskell Simpson, Assistant General Passenger Agent for the line and in charge of Santa Fe advertising operations for more than twenty-two years, to lure a nation full of potential customers by instilling an image of "the people's kind of railroad," a marketing ploy that would reverse the lingering impression of a railroad that only served "Land Hunters, Buffalo Hunters, and Gold Hunters."[6]

Simpson's boyhood years were spent in Lawrence, Kansas, and upon graduation from college in 1880 he took a job as an advertising clerk in the Santa Fe's general passenger department at Topeka. In 1900, he became general manager and executive of Santa Fe's promotional operations. Simpson directed what one publication, *The Santa Fe New Mexican*, described as "the most elaborate, ambitious and effective program of development-publicity ever inaugurated by any railroad." "Advertising Art" was developed in this country for the first time in a big way. "I think that we were the first road in the land to take art seriously, as a valuable advertising adjunct," Simpson told an interviewer. "We have never skimped. We use the very best art that can be bought and we reproduce it in the very best way that it can be reproduced." "And yet, after all," he continued, "we do not wish to take ourselves too seriously. . . . At least we are not afraid to do the new things."[7]

The "new things" had begun in the 1890s, when Santa Fe executives brought a number of famous painters to their Southwest territories. In 1892, the railroad commissioned the distinguished artist Thomas Moran to paint the Grand Canyon in return for transportation, food, and lodging. It was an astonishing and epic work. The Santa Fe Railway reproduced *Grand Canyon* as a six-color lithograph and distributed thousands of copies throughout the country.

It was just at this time that the railway began to recognize the unique possibilities it possessed for the artist. Charles F. Lummis, an author and a keen enthusiast for Western American Art and the untouched realms of nature in the Southwest, wrote, "It was an accident that the Santa Fe route, when it followed the line of least resistance across 'the Great American Desert' . . . skimmed the cream of the artist's interest of the Southwest. There is no railroad in the world . . . which penetrates such a wonderland of the pictorial in geography and in humanity."[8] That same year, Fernand Lungren, another painter of renown, was invited by the Santa Fe to sketch and paint for one of their advertising campaigns, and his career as a Western painter took off. He would devote his life to painting scenes of the Southwest desert.

Simpson was himself an ardent admirer of art and literature, and very early he understood the importance of the picturesque as a vital means of attracting tourists to the Southwest. Under his aegis, other painters were to follow. In 1906, the pattern of commissioning artists was given a dramatic impetus when Simpson persuaded William R. Leigh to come West. Leigh was legendary as a painter and illustrator and was known as the "Sagebrush Rembrandt." He had been infatuated with the West since early boyhood and spoke for many of his contemporaries when he recalled this desire. "From the moment I returned from my studies in Europe, I had wanted to go West, which I had already determined was really true America, and what I wanted to paint. I made many efforts to that end, but was always troubled by lack of funds and misinformation as to the cost and difficulties."[9] Leigh specialized in cowboy life and frontier scenes and painted the Grand Canyon with thundering results. The experience was a turning point for Leigh. He declared that "Never in the whole of human history, at any time or anywhere, has there been a terrain more suitable for making of pictures or telling of stories."[10] The Santa Fe bought five of his paintings to display in their hotels and to publicize their new branch lines.

In 1907, the Santa Fe introduced an annual calendar that was circulated gratis through what must have then been one of the largest general mailings in advertising history. What the artist did for the landscape, the Santa Fe calendar did for the Indian. The calendar alerted the public to the existence of the railroad and of Indian culture in the Southwest. The calendar had a predominantly Indian theme, generally romantic, that was illustrated by original works from the newly established Taos and Santa Fe artists' colonies. Hundreds of thousands of calendars found their way into schools, businesses, households, and onto Santa Fe Railway stockholders' walls. The "Santa Fe Indian," who dominated the calendar, came into being. This Indian possessed an aura of glamour. An intangibility. An ineffable essence. The idea was to present a radiant image of Indian life.

The Santa Fe Indian represented a prototype of preindustrial society. Simplicity. Freedom. Nobility. This was the life and culture that inhabited the Santa Fe's "friendly" oasis of the desert Southwest. In dire need of a powerful symbol to catch the public's imagination, the Santa Fe appropriated the Indian and his culture to establish for itself a meaningful emblem that would galvanize the American imagination. Its calendar images and the names the Santa Fe borrowed from Indian culture to christen their trains (for example, the "Chief," the "Navajo," and the "Super Chief") provided the public with instant and easy identification with Indians. The adoption of the Indian proved to be an important step for the Santa Fe Railway in its synthesis of corporate image making and primitive culture.[11] Although not an explicit part of the Santa Fe's advertising goals, its promotional themes transformed the Indians into symbolic reductions of the American heritage. The success of that enterprise sprang from the American public's longing for belonging, its quest for roots, and its unconscious desire for liberation from a violent past.

The creative synthesis of business interests and culture by the Santa Fe Railway was a unique application of modern advertising techniques. The campaign centered on the patriotic: a call to get to know one's country. The railway's advertising images of the landscape and the Indian were glazed with beauty and picturesqueness, promoting "a last refuge of magic, mountains and quaint ancestors." But they also evoked a sense of mythological place—a distant West as a land filled with natural wonders, with the promise of a whole new set of different experiences implying a "rite of passage" from the familiar East to the wild, exotic, and slightly dangerous West, where "normal" rules don't apply. The pictures had a refreshing and tantalizing effect. These technicolor fantasies were to become a source of the railway's advertising power. Their impact on the public was enormous.

Since the primary concern of the Santa Fe Railway was to attract passenger and freight traffic, one would not expect its advertising department to address the complexities of the people and the land the railroad was promoting. However, in assuming the cultural legacy of the American Indian, the admen gave the impression that they were a knowledgeable "ethnographic authority," confidently imposing themselves on another culture by encapsulating it both in image and aphorism. Though the Santa Fe knew little about the meaning and function of the cultures it was portraying, it was able to create emblematic and striking images of Southwest Indian life. The railroad found a way of successfully integrating these images into its own designs for corporate self-enhancement and growth and for the selling of the West to tourists and settlers. These advertising images were displayed in widely circulated calendars, posters, brochures, timetables, magazine and newspaper ads. In this way, the Santa Fe Railway encouraged the tourist to feel that he was discovering a vital part of his heritage.

The Santa Fe's publicity policy was tremendously successful. It became its most valuable cargo. It enabled the railroad to establish the national identity it was so earnestly seeking. The Santa Fe's rhetoric of belonging fell into place, and the railroad's "Americanization" of the Indian began.

Nationalism, culture, intentional fantasy, and the romance of the West—these were the foundations upon which the promotional strategies of the Santa Fe advertising department were built. The Santa Fe admen undoubtedly sensed the common elements in the romance of railroading and the romance of the American Indian. The blend of the two led inevitably to powerful copy. The *Zeitgeist* of exploring new territories and unknown cultures provided ample source material for the image makers. Railroad novels were a contemporary genre describing great adventures of railroading seen from the point of view of the engineers and the road builders. "Anthropological" accounts of Indian life appeared regularly in magazines and newspapers.[12]

The thrill of new places and exotic but native cultures were central themes of the Santa Fe's promotion of the Southwest. In advancing those themes, the Santa Fe's approach was "folksy by instinct, foxy by interest," combined with shrewd business practice. The romantic railway illustrations offer a strange and splendid harmony, suggesting untold tales of America. They convey an atmosphere of endless excitement, adventure, and exotica, with an emphasis on the simple life of nature, appealing strongly to the Byronic element, against mechanical routine. The Santa Fe posters became the most talked-of illustrations in advertising circles on the Pacific coast. They were different, unlike anything that had appeared before. A "poster genius" had been found and was promptly hidden away from predatory competitors. To this day, the creator of many of these distinctive, powerful, and popular illustrations remains unknown.

In addition to the posters, lavish brochures, lithographs, folders, annual calendars, magic-lantern slide shows, and maps (small and large and "a million or more each year") revealed a spectacular display of artistic wizardry.[13] Travel lectures with a magic-lantern show were a popular item on trains, in schools and universities and businesses. They were often accompanied by ten-minute movie shorts displaying some aspect of the culture or land through which the Santa Fe traversed. Travel kits comprising slides and film were provided by the railroad to their lecturers and photographers as a very effective means of advertising their line. A sampling of such lantern slides and film forms a major part of this book.

The artist and the photographer each contributed significantly to the successful campaign of the railroad to shape public interest in the Southwest and thereby to grab as large a share as possible of the tourist and freight traffic for which it was competing. Each of their contributions deserves special scrutiny.

The images created by the railroad's artists and photographers differed in a number of important respects. The well-established tradition of painting gave the artist unlimited possibilities for representing and interpreting his subject matter. On the other hand, the relatively new discipline of photography would render that same subject matter with considerably less variation. What emerged were two fundamentally different kinds of

The Chief
is still Chief—

the **Chief**
is still Chief

Santa Fe

Extra Fast
Extra Fine
Extra Fare

5 hours faster

FROM
PAINTING
BY
GERALD CASSIDY

The **Chief**
is Chief

the **Chief**
is still chief—

fastest and only extra
fare train to
Southern California

No extra fare on the Santa Fe's six other daily California trains

Extra fast
Extra fine
Extra fare

Fred Harvey dining service is a distinctive feature of this distinctive railway.

The Indian-detour — Grand Canyon Line

W. J. Black, Pass. Traffic Mgr. Santa Fe System, 1210 Railway Exchange, Chicago Ill.
Am interested in winter trip to_____ Please send detailed information and descriptive folders.

**mail
this
coupon**

Name_____ Address_____

Reprinted from the November 1929 issues of The Big 4 Group

the Indian-detour

The America of Coronado waits for you beside this motor trail —

An enchanted land, where for three days your luxurious Harveycar carries you on a personally-escorted tour of ancient Indian pueblos and prehistoric cliff-dwellings in the New Mexico Rockies between Las Vegas, Santa Fé and Albuquerque.

A new motor link in the Santa Fe cross-continent rail journey to and from California. Only $80, with everything provided, meals, accommodations with bath every night and motor transportation.

Extended Motor Land Cruises by Harveycar can be arranged at any time to penetrate most any part of the Santa Fe Southwest. Rates are by the day and include car expense, meals and accommodations, private courier service and driver.

Indian-detours
~ Most distinctive Motor Cruise service in the world ~~~~

back through the centuries

the Indian-detour

Bulletin No.1
February 1927

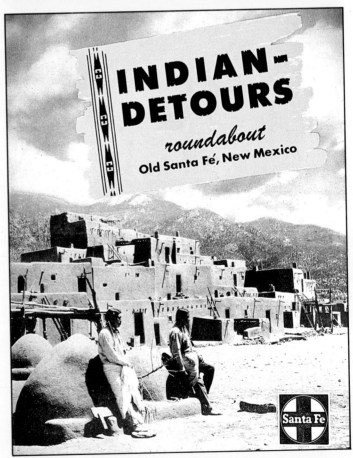

INDIAN-DETOURS
roundabout
Old Santa Fé, New Mexico

portraits of Indian life. Another difference, of a temporary nature, also exerted a significant influence on the photographic images used by the Santa Fe. At its inception, in 1839, photography was limited to black-and-white images, even though the desirability of color was recognized by its founders. Since practical techniques for the commercial production of color photographs were not available until the 1930s, it was necessary to turn to other methods for rendering colored photographic images. Each of the colored photographic lantern slides that are reproduced in this book is the product of the long-standing craft of transforming black-and-white photographs into hand-colored images.

THE CALENDAR ART OF THE SANTA FE RAILWAY

This South-west, which is but one chapter of our rich tradition, is our own authentic wonderland—a treasure-trove of romantic myth—profoundly significant and beautiful, guarded by ancient races practicing their ancient rites, in a region of incredible color and startling natural grandeur.

Harriet Monroe (1920)[1]

The calendar paintings and poster and brochure illustrations of the Santa Fe Railway had about them the lingering air of another time. They are dramatic evidence of the powerful narcotic that nostalgia is capable of being. These images stirred the imagination and played a central role in the selling of the Southwest and Indian culture to the American public. The paintings acquired by the Santa Fe appeared in the railroad's large waiting rooms, in new branch offices, in hotels along the line, and in national and international exhibitions.

The Santa Fe imagery was wholly consistent with popular thinking about society, politics, and patriotic themes. In 1906, at a conference opened by President Theodore Roosevelt, J. Horace McFarland, then president of the American Civic Association, urged Americans "to consider the essential value of one of America's greatest resources—her unmatched natural scenery," pointing out that "the true glory of the United States must rest, and has rested, upon a deeper foundation than that of her purely material resources. It is the love of the country that lights and keeps glowing the holy fire of patriotism. And this love is excited primarily by the beauty of the country."[2]

Since 1898, painters, playwrights, poets, and writers from every region of the United States have traveled to Sante Fe and Taos. Awed and stimulated by the astonishing natural scenery, the early arrivals stayed and established what was to become a well-known and flourishing artists' colony, one that would create acceptability for this previously unknown area of America. They were attracted to the region because of its remoteness and great beauty, its spectacular landscape and salubrious climate, and its exotic blend of American Indian and Hispanic cultures. All were seeking "fresh material" and felt the need for a new "stimulating subject." Ernest L. Blumenschein, one of the founders of the Taos colony, spoke for many when he expressed his feelings upon first seeing the land in 1898: "When I came into this valley—for the first time in my life, I saw whole paintings right before my eyes. Everywhere I looked I saw paintings perfectly organized, ready for paint."[3]

The enchantment was instant. The light dazzled and the sky was "so brilliant that it vibrate[d]." The "brightness and clarity" captivated nearly all the artists. Continues Blumenschein: "We all drifted into Taos like skilled hands looking for a steady job. We found it, as it grew into an urge that pushed us to our limits, a joyous inspiration to produce and give to the deepest extent of each man's own calibre. We lived only to paint. And that is what happened to every artist who passed this way!"[4]

Leo Stein, a well-known art collector and brother of Gertrude, visited Taos in 1916 and was equally entranced. He exclaimed: " . . . [I] had never known such beauty on earth except in early Chinese paintings, and [I] had never believed it could live outside of art."[5]

The Santa Fe and Taos artists were seeking a rebirth of spirit and an alternative to urban culture. Bored by the European painterly tradition, they began to look to their own roots in an attempt to feed themselves from American soil and to establish something that could be called "truly American." New Mexico offered the restorative power, the regeneration of spirit, that these artists were seeking. Many of the artists drew creative

flashing *with color*
sparkling *with sunshine*

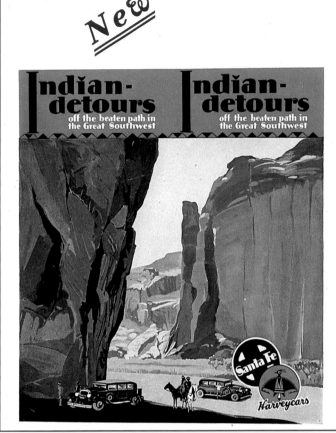

New

Indian-detours
off the beaten path in the Great Southwest

Indian-detours
off the beaten path in the Great Southwest

Santa Fe
Harveycars

Santa Fe
Harveycars

the **Indian-detour**

Bulletin No 2   August 1927

Gallup, New Mexico
The Land of Enchantment
invites you to attend its
Inter-Tribal Indian Ceremonial
September 10·11·12 1924

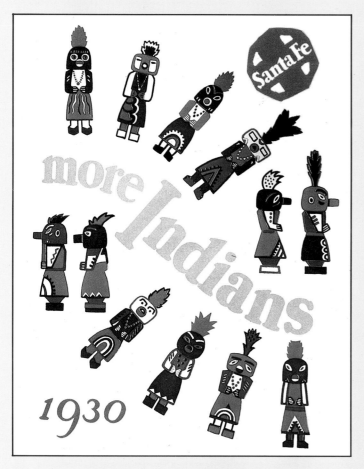

more Indians

1930

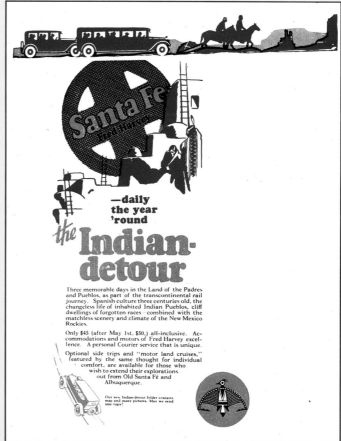

—daily the year 'round

the Indian-detour

Three memorable days in the Land of the Padres and Pueblos, as part of the transcontinental rail journey. Spanish culture three centuries old, the changeless life of inhabited Indian Pueblos, cliff dwellings of forgotten races—combined with the matchless scenery and climate of the New Mexico Rockies.

Only $45 (after May 1st, $50.) all-inclusive. Accommodations and motors of Fred Harvey excellence. A personal Courier service that is unique.

Optional side trips and "motor land cruises," featured by the same thought for individual comfort, are available for those who wish to extend their explorations out from Old Santa Fé and Albuquerque.

Our new Indian-detour folder contains map and many pictures. May we send you copy?

1928

more Indians

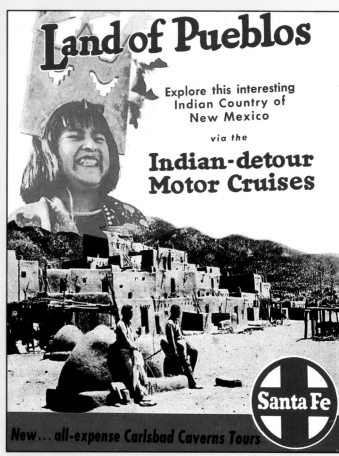

Land of Pueblos

Explore this interesting Indian Country of New Mexico

via the

Indian-detour Motor Cruises

Santa Fe

New... all-expense Carlsbad Caverns Tours

A Santa Fe Railway calendar with one of the Indian paintings

and spiritual nourishment not only from their newly established proximity to the land but also from their contact with Pueblo culture. These cultures were *of* the American soil.

The Pueblo Indian and his life emerged as important themes in the work of some of these artists. The attraction was twofold. The Indians' unity with their natural environment as expressed through their religious ceremonials and daily life stirred the spirit and aroused the curiosity of the artist. In addition, their colorful and picturesque appearance and strange and exotic customs provided a strong visual stimulus. From the artists' point of view, the Pueblo Indian lived in a land of timelessness and had an "aura of innocence" about him. It was a fresh new universe for the painters.

Ernest L. Blumenschein was enchanted with the Indians he saw, describing them as "picturesque, colorful, dressed in blankets artistically draped." E. Irving Couse, another Taos founder, considered the "copper skinned"[6] Pueblo Indians aesthetically pleasing and spent most of his life painting them. Couse heard about Taos from Blumenschein and Bert Greer Phillips. Their enthusiasm for the region was unrivaled after their first visit there in 1898. All three had trained under the "academic discipline" of the Académie Julian in Paris. Won over by their descriptions, Couse arrived in Taos in 1902.

Phillips, who had set out with Blumenschein in 1898 to tour the Southwest, decided to stay the moment he laid eyes on Taos. Mesmerized by the natural beauty and ethnic charm of the region, he devoted the rest of his life to recording it on canvas. He was particularly impressed with the strong sense of myth that imbued Indian life. On one occasion he marveled: "As I visit their villages and talk with my Indian friends, I see and hear the young bucks wrapped in their white blankets standing on the bridge singing a love song in the moonlight, and I feel the romance of youth. . . . I believe it is the romance of this great pure-aired land that makes the most lasting impression on my mind and heart."[7] Thus, the Indian became a popular theme in the paintings of these talented artists, even though they knew little about the culture they were "capturing."

The spirit that animates their work is genuine enough. The artists' subjects were portrayed in their natural landscape, where their lives were infused with a profound harmony with nature. Their images are an affirmation of sympathy with Indian life. These artists were, however, lacking in any apparent awareness of the particularities of the culture they were representing. They painted what they *felt* and what they *wanted* to feel. The Taos and Santa Fe painters revealed, as Poe said the true artist should, "a wild effort to reach the beauty above."[8]

The artist Paul Burlin spoke for them all when he expressed his own ambivalence and lack of experience—but attraction nonetheless. "My introduction to the art of the Indian stirred up strange conflicts. I was ignorant of the Indian and knew nothing of his work. And since I didn't know him, I feared him, although I wanted to know how he lived and what he did. I traveled to distant places to learn; I heard his chants. . . . I was entranced with his witch doctors and the whole aspect of the metaphysical propitiation of the forces of nature."[9]

It is not surprising that this mixture often gave rise to pastoral scenes of Biblical peace and plenty, for it was, in fact, precisely these aspects of life the artists were seeking. The quality of native life, with its bond to the earth and elemental primitiveness, was a palpable force that the artists found hard to resist.

By the end of the first decade of this century, the Indians began to pose as models for the artists, and the artists became spokesmen of a new epoch, leading *The Los Angeles Times* to proclaim that the Santa Fe and Taos art colonies show "the world that we have an art native to our soil . . . [and that] the Indian and his pueblo are subjects well worthy of exploitation."[10] Another writer set the stage for the Santa Fe Railway's image makers. Commenting upon an exhibition by the Santa Fe artist Theodore Van Soelen, he wrote presciently: " . . . few have the 'allure' of those of Van Soelen. . . . Van Soelen actually 'sells' the place to us. If reproductions of the pictures were used on railway time-tables, the trains to Santa Fe, Taos, etc, would be far more crowded than they are at present."[11]

William H. Simpson, an advertising executive of the Santa Fe, was enthusiastic about the artists in Taos and Santa Fe, and he commissioned work that dramatized the idea of the Far West and the Indian. These artists evoked a sense of place as vividly as did the Romantic poets in their writings of their European travels. This gave rise to our modern rhetoric of nature. All of the painters developed an attitude of mind toward the West—and the Indian in particular—one infused with the same romantic motives that governed the work of James Fenimore Cooper and made his *Leatherstocking Tales* so successful. It was this romantic inheritance that the artists turned to and that the railroad promoted.

Virtually each year, from 1907 until the present, the Santa Fe calendar has featured a different Indian scene painted by one of the artists from New Mexico. The Indian pictures were especially commissioned by Simpson, who managed and nourished the railroad's relationship with these artists. The Santa Fe Indian was soon to replace the wild warrior, the plainsman, and the railroader in the forefront of romantic thought.

The images used by the railway's advertising department were carefully planned to convey a specific cultural message. The Santa Fe's Indian is a dignified and proud warrior. Simpson and the railway clearly strove for the heroic qualities and a sense of the legendary, displaying an aloof indifference to actuality. Their focus was the dignity of the "old-time Indian" that everyone has read or dreamed about. (Simpson's own poetry reflects this attitude.)[12] They understood the value of sentimentalizing the romantic features of Indian culture and the effect that such images would have on an impressionable public, particularly tourists.

The Santa Fe calendar images of Indian life are a fascinating excursion into the world of popular decoration. These images constituted a universe of stereotypes that served as compelling ornaments on the kitchen wall of the typical American household. In this respect, the railway's calendar-art depiction of American Indian life shows us a culture that has no history. Clearly, it would have been counterproductive to do otherwise. The pictures do not speak of the countless losses and diminishments that the Indians experienced in their futile struggle to hold on to their native lands. Rather, their history is passed over in silence.

The artists Simpson chose to work with had a predisposition to view things, in the words of Mark Twain, through the "mellow moonshine of romance." This vision, although conceptually limited, was the one that best suited the needs of railway advertising. The approach conveyed verisimilitude and the paintings resonated with the spirit of the time.

Top left: E. Irving Couse, The War Shield, *1914. Top right: E. Irving Couse*, Taos Turkey Hunters, *1916. Bottom left: J. H. Sharp,*
Old War Bonnet, *1916. Bottom right: E. Irving Couse*, The Turquoise Bead Maker, *1925*

The canvases which Simpson solicited were expected to be "thematically pleasing and colorfully decorative" and neither "pictorially perplexing" nor "intellectually challenging." Ultimately, what was produced by the advertising department of the Santa Fe was a magnification of the railway's sense of popular taste.[13] Simpson offered suggestions not only for the artistic content (subject matter) of the paintings but also for the actual rendering of the painting itself. This was perhaps one of the first instances in which the corporate executive and the artist worked in concert to achieve such a popular mass image.

Of all the artists whom Simpson employed, he favored E. Irving Couse for many of the calendar scenes. In fact, Couse's paintings were the first to appear on the calendar in 1914 and were showcased without interruption from 1916 to 1938. Couse's images are icons frozen in time. They embody the world of the archetype—the poetic ideals of simplicity, nobility, and innocence that were thought to be found where man is close to nature. Clearly, Couse's romantic vision was sincerely inspired by his exotic and picturesque surroundings. But like a great many of his colleagues,

Walter Ufer, Taos Girls, *1916*

his infatuation and fascination with his subject matter and the mythical characteristics that it inspired brought a magnificently unreal aspect to his work. It was lyrical and escapist in tone. However, it was that much more powerful *because* of its lyricism, and it hooked the imagination.

Simpson often participated in Couse's execution of a canvas. He would suggest alterations that would make the work more suitable for the purposes of the railway's advertising policy. He sometimes wrote detailed instructions to Couse, such as the following: "Assume that in the finished paintings you will get plenty of light on the hair of the two figures, as well as on the dark blue dress of the woman. It would seem that the olla, the metate, the buckskin leggins on the man and his head dress afford special opportunity for the brilliant white effect mentioned in previous correspondence. The strong white gives a sparkle to the picture, which is very attractive for calendar use."[14]

Simpson loved a campfire atmosphere and would propose background changes on this theme: " . . . am wondering about what the effect would be if this [picture] were to be made a firelight scene as well."[15] Couse's first calendar painting for Simpson was a campfire scene in front of which he posed a crouching and barely clad Indian (*Wal-si-el, Good Medicine*). He used the campfire motif throughout his work. It would become

Bert Greer Phillips, The Secret Olla, *1918*

almost a signature, along with his crouching Indian figures. Throughout their long and highly successful working relationship, Simpson continued to propose subject changes and Couse would comply. Simpson went so far as to experiment with some of the sketches that Couse submitted as calendar possibilities. Consider the following advice: "Note that we have experimented by pasting on a slip to see how it would look if the warbonnet was made larger. Rather like the effect, and wish you would kindly correct the sketch accordingly. While the face is attractive and out of the ordinary, [we] . . . feel that *it might look a little more like the Indian Chief most of us have in our mind* if following changes were made. . . . " [italics added.][16]

   In a discussion with Couse about a particular calendar image, *The Chief*, Simpson inadvertently sets forth his impressions of what the prototype of an Indian ought to look like. This correspondence gives us a rare and direct glimpse into one facet of corporate image-making. He wrote: "The figure of the Chief doesn't look quite tall enough for one entitled to that name. Perhaps the 'squattiness' may be due to the war bonnet being so wide, or possibly to the way the blanket hangs. No doubt you can overcome this when working from the model."[17] Simpson signed off:

Bert Greer Phillips, Taos Indian, *1907*

"Please return sketch with face worked over. . . . You are on the right track. . . . The above suggestions are only from the advertising and not artistic viewpoint. . . ."[18] Couse returned his sketch a month later "with corrections as suggested."[19]

Simpson's ideas were taken seriously and the "partnership" between business executive and artist succeeded in injecting a commercial ethic in the artistic endeavors of a significant number of Taos and Santa Fe painters. The Santa Fe trademark was prominently and artistically displayed in each picture commissioned ("Leave room for it to be put into the sky afterwards when the lithographing is done," wrote Simpson to Couse).[20] The paintings, in turn, made the artists and Indians known to millions.

E. Irving Couse's work fit the Santa Fe Railway's mold, as did that of several other Taos artists. For Simpson's needs, Couse was a "visual stenographer," posing his Indians and infusing his scenes with the romantic impulse. Couse removed the Indian from his cultural context and created an "unrelated" Indian. His Indians are irresistible, gentle, quiet ghosts of former beings, curiously unreal and dreamlike. A condition of innocence pervades all his work.

Walter Ufer, another Taos artist, whose work was also purchased by Simpson for the calendar, was, like Couse, a painter of tremendous talent who enjoyed considerable financial success. He sold a reported $150,000 worth of paintings in three years by turning out the same picture over and over, an Indian on a white horse posed against a Taos mountain looming in the background.[21]

Couse, too, was immensely successful with his calendar images. They catapulted him, overnight, into national recognition. But his colleagues scorned him for his commercialism and accused him of pandering to the unformed opinions of an uninformed public. They also complained of his lack of taste. Blumenschein ridiculed his predictable choice of subjects and his lack of artistic enterprise, saying Couse "painted an Indian squatting before a buffalo hide on which he was drawing." He continued, ". . . that painting . . . made him famous and he has been painting the same squatting Indian ever since."[22]

THE GREAT AMERICAN AMALGAM: TECHNOLOGY AND CULTURE

Into what currency
have they changed our singing?
John Berger[1]

With the daguerreotype everyone will be able to have their portrait taken—formerly it was only the prominent; and at the same time everything is being done to make us all look exactly the same—so that we shall only need one portrait.
Kierkegaard (1854)[2]

The Golden Era of railroading overlapped considerably with the Golden Era of photography. Both set the stage and paved the way for the modern tourist. In addition to using paintings and illustrations, the Santa Fe Railway extended its campaign for a monopoly of the tourist market by circulating grand and enchanting photographic images of Indian life and the scenery of the Southwest to advertise its lines, to encourage settlement, to attract tourists, and simply to generate excitement. This was achieved by contracting for the services of a wide variety of professional, commercial, and amateur photographers.

Conservatively, one would estimate that there must have been hundreds of photographers in the employ of the Santa Fe Railway during the formative years of its advertising program. Regrettably, we know the names of but a handful of the corps of photographers who produced images of Southwest life under the aegis of the railroad. Given photography's uncertain and youthful status as an art form, photographers of that time were less likely than modern photographers to credit themselves as the creators of particular photographs. Authorship also got lost in the shuffle of the mass production of images.

Many of the photographs the railroad purchased were colored by other artists or by coloring firms. Other photographs were severely cropped to fit the rectangular format of the magic-lantern slide. In general, the railroad felt free to modify photographic images so that they conformed to the requirements of its promotional themes for postcards and lantern slides.

The work of nine identifiable photographers appears in this book. These photographers are by no means a homogeneous group. Some were serious amateurs (Fay Cooper Cole and Aaron B. Craycraft). Several had well-established reputations as scenic and portrait photographers (W. H. Jackson, Jesse Nausbaum, and A. C. Vromans); others used photography as a vital adjunct to their business interests (William E. Kopplin and W. H. Simpson, advertising; Edward H. Kemp, lantern slides; Fred Harvey, tourism). The following four individuals are representative of the range of photographers whose work was used by the advertising department of the Santa Fe Railway.

William Henry Jackson

Of the known photographers whose work appears in this book, the most renowned is William Henry Jackson. Jackson was retained by nearly every major railroad in the United States to take scenic views along their routes. During the 1880s and 1890s, railroad photography became his chief line of business. Writing about his beginnings in *The Philadelphia Photographer*, Jackson recalled: "Portrait photography never had a chance for me, so I sought my subjects from the housetops, and finally the hilltops and about the surrounding country. . . . The opening of the Pacific Railroad in 1869 render[ed] easy access [to] a region rich in scenic effects and interest, [and] I determined to photograph it."[3] Jackson called his first promotional work for the railroads "landscape photography or viewing."[4]

"We'll provide a private car and ten dollars a photograph,"[5] said the publicity representative of the Baltimore and Ohio Railroad, in an offer to Jackson in 1892. Nothing was spared. Jackson, as did many other railroad photographers, traveled lavishly in specially equipped cars that included a front "parlor," a fully serviced darkroom, and living quarters for the photographer and his assistant. Jackson's collection of railroad pictures numbered approximately thirty thousand and spanned a period of nearly fifteen years. Jackson always maintained that he was "in quest of the picturesque and marvelous. . . . Scenes of amazing grandeur lured me," he once said.[6] His majestic Western vistas, such as his panoramic views of Yosemite and Yellowstone, are legendary. Jackson also photographed the Indians of the Southwest. Examples of his Indian work include *Shipaulovi, Moki Pueblo*, page 91, *Hopi Harvest Dance*, page 112, and *Pueblo of Taos, New Mexico*, page 163.

As a commercial photographer who was also highly skilled as a retoucher and colorist, Jackson's first impulse was to produce a salable image. His flair for the theatrical is demonstrated in what one historian of photography described as his "composite paste-up and paint-in world."[7] He thought nothing of adding to and subtracting from a photograph as long as his alterations succeeded in strengthening a particular image. Jackson's Detroit Publishing Company turned out reproductions of millions of his hand-colored images as photographs and as postcards. Jackson loved color. He was called the "Father of the Picture Postcard." As was common of photographers of that period, his wife assisted him as a colorist. Jackson frequently presented "lecture tours" which consisted of illustrated talks on the places and countries he had visited, using his own lantern slides to promote his own work. One such talk, which he gave throughout the state of Colorado, was called "One Hundred Minutes in Strange Lands" and was illustrated with 125 hand-colored slides.[8] He also toured the Southwest on board the Santa Fe's "California Special," giving informal talks while projecting his work.[9]

Edward H. Kemp

Edward H. Kemp was an entrepreneur and amateur photographer who had his own lantern-slide business in San Francisco. He made, sold, and traded in lantern-slide views. He was a member of the Amateur Photographers Association, the "California Camera Club," and he contributed

INTERIOR OF W.H. JACKSON'S PHOTOGRAPHIC RAILWAY CAR ON BOARD THE CALIFORNIA LIMITED

articles to *Camera Craft* magazine. Kemp and his wife took a special interest in the Hopi villages of Arizona and made several trips there to photograph the Snake Dance. By the time of one of their visits, in 1905, the Snake Dance had already become a popular attraction for photographer and tourist alike. The presence of both, however, was becoming a serious threat to the devout meaning of the ritual. Columns of photographers jockeyed for the best camera positions as the tourists poured onto the small mesa plaza. Mrs. Kemp noted that she and her husband were obliged to station themselves in a "photographer's row," a special spot designated for camera users.[10]

The Snake Dance and the Grand Canyon were promoted heavily by the Santa Fe, and Kemp photographed both for his own business and for the railroad. Other examples of Kemp's work include *The Grand Canyon, The Diamond Hitch*, page 66, top, *Phantom Ranch, Grand Canyon*, page 67, and *Crystal Trading Post, General View*, page 52. As far as one can tell, all of Kemp's original negatives were destroyed in the San Francisco earthquake and fire of 1906. Thus all that remains of his work are isolated prints and lantern slides.

William Ernest Kopplin

At the age of twenty-five, in 1907, William Ernest Kopplin left Racine, Wisconsin, and went to Chicago to work for the Santa Fe Railway in its advertising department. Early in his career, he developed a passionate interest in Indian culture, which persisted throughout his life. Known by his colleagues as "a real live wire in advertising efficiency," Kopplin spent much of his time riding the rails as a "lanternist" promoting the line.[11] His lantern lectures were set up on board the trains to inform tourists of the unique scenery and services of the Santa Fe line. Kopplin traveled extensively throughout the Southwest photographing the Hopi and Navajo Indians of Arizona and the Pueblos of New Mexico. He was also an accomplished cameraman, putting this skill to use when he filmed the Hopi Snake Dance for the railway in 1912. This footage is unusually rare. A detailed description appears on pages 131–142.

One interesting and significant feature of Kopplin's work reveals the influence of his status as an employee of the Santa Fe Railway. In order to assuage fears that potential tourists might have of traveling through Indian territory, many of his photographs included the reassuring presence of tourists and other photographers photographing Indians. (See *Estufa, San Ildefonso, New Mexico*, page 167, *War Dance, Zuni Pueblo*, page 185, and *Edge of the Mesa, After the Snake Dance*, page 143.)

Fred Harvey

Fred Harvey, the least renowned photographer of this group, is more generally recognized as an extraordinarily successful entrepreneur of food, hotel, and sightseeing services along the Santa Fe Railway. Even though he did not spend as much time personally producing photographs as did Jackson, Kemp, and Kopplin, he contributed significantly to the advertising interests of the Santa Fe by hiring other photographers. Indeed, the Santa Fe's commercial interests were so central to Fred Harvey's career that failure to mention him and his enterprises in a book about the Santa Fe Railway would constitute a glaring omission.

In 1904, the Santa Fe built the El Tovar hotel on the rim of the Grand Canyon. Here, Harvey housed H. E. McAvoy, his official Canyon photographer, in a specially equipped studio. The photographer's sole responsibility was to catch the Canyon in all its splendor for the tourist, traveler, and the advertising purposes of the Santa Fe. Another of Harvey's specialists at the Canyon, Pete Peters, known as "Pete the Wonder," would then hand-color every photograph.[12] Peters' brushwork was greatly and widely admired. A sampling of his impressive and delicate coloring may be seen in *Grand Canyon Vista*, page 63. His sensitive tinting gives rhythm to the whole and establishes a fine balance of tone. This is particularly difficult to achieve with such an unearthly spectacle as the Canyon.

Contemplating the Canyon is comparable to watching an endless sunset. At different times of day, the Canyon is awash with kaleidoscopic shifts of color, which cast a surreal effect. Thus, *any* rendering tends to be at unsettling odds with the credible. William E. Kopplin's hand-colored image of the Canyon (page 60) exemplifies the problem of finding a tenable way of expressing this feast of color. As audacious an interpretation as it may seem, it is, nonetheless, real.

Fred Harvey took pictures himself. One of his favorites was *A Corn Dancer*, page 186. He also employed other photographers to cover the points of interest skirting the Santa Fe line. Indian ceremonials were important as a tourist attraction and his Canyon and Indian pictures prettified the railway brochures, timetables, and folders and romanced the public.

It is important to recognize that Fred Harvey's history of romancing the public had its roots in an extensive career of providing a broad range of tourist services along the Santa Fe Railway. Harvey had emigrated from England and worked as a freight agent for one of the Eastern railroads in the 1870s. Because of his extensive travels, he knew a lot about the miserable and dirty lunchrooms along the railway routes. The food was unpalatable and prices were outrageous. The railroad dining car had not yet come into existence, and the problem of feeding the travelers who were beginning to cross the prairies in great numbers became acute. Harvey saw what was needed, and in 1876, he approached the Santa Fe with a new concept in railroad dining: He would provide good food in clean surroundings at moderate prices! The railway decided to take a chance with him. That same year, Harvey opened his first lunchroom on the second floor of the Santa Fe station at Topeka. A wonderful and varied menu (roast veal, chicken, halibut, sweetbreads, and spring lamb, for $1.00 each), spotless surroundings, Irish linen tablecloths, and Sheffield silver plate astonished passengers and local citizenry alike. Harvey also brought glamour to the West with his famed Harvey Girls, young ladies from good families who served as waitresses. Wearing long black dresses, flowing white aprons, and hairbows, they became legend. Before joining, they had to promise not to marry for a year. The turnover was tremendous.

In late 1876, Harvey opened his first hotel, Harvey House, at Florence, Kansas, on the Santa Fe. The effect was sensational and the response was electric. Harvey Houses soon stretched from Chicago to California. Typically, the railroad would build them and the Fred Harvey Company would design, furnish, and operate them. The Fred Harvey Company became an enterprise that provided food, hotel, and sightseeing services along the Santa Fe Railway. When dining cars were added to the Santa Fe line, Fred Harvey set up the service. Local color and historical background were key elements in the decor of each Harvey undertaking. Authentic Indian and Spanish architecture and art dominated, adorned, and charmed. A special attraction of several Harvey hotels was the Lecture Lounge. At La Fonda Hotel in Santa Fe, for example, the tourist was treated to informal talks that featured lantern slides and moving pictures about the Pueblo Indians and the history and geography of the Southwest.

The Santa Fe Railway felt that what the public needed were palpable images that would help them grasp the reality of Western lands and that would also ameliorate the menacing image that the railway's potential customers had of America's vast tracts of desert. To a large extent that need was met by the railroad's scenic photography and by its images of Pueblo culture. A new development in photography also facilitated the Santa Fe's efforts to attract tourists. American families, at the turn of the century, began to take up photography for themselves through mass-produced and inexpensive Kodaks. ("You press the button; we do the rest!") This development produced an interesting and unexpected dividend. Many of the first tourists to the Southwest brought with them their new Kodaks and showed no inhibition about using them (see *Edge of the Mesa, after the Snake Dance*, page 143). In 1906, an editorial writer commented:

> About half the tourists jump from the trains almost as soon as they stop and run from one place to another in search of souvenir postal cards, flop themselves down in the waiting-room or on the brick curb and write feverishly, hunt around for some place to buy stamps and then mail their cards, and by that time have only a few minutes left to patronize the lunch counter. Meanwhile, the greater portion of the other half are taking snapshots of the hotel or station, or are posing against one of the buildings for someone else's picture. It's as good as a circus to watch them.[13]

Travel would never be the same.

THE AGE OF THE MAGIC LANTERN: ADVENTUROUS INTERLUDES IN LIFE AND COLOR

As a matter of fact, our great-grandfathers, who never went anywhere, in actuality had more experience of the world than we have who have seen everything. When they listened to a lecture with lantern slides, they really held their breath before the unknown, as they sat in the village school-room.

D. H. Lawrence (1929)[1]

With color one obtains an energy that seems to stem from witchcraft.
Henri Matisse (1905)[2]

Invented in the middle of the seventeenth century, the magic lantern foreshadowed contemporary motion-picture technology.[3] It evolved into what Edison described as "an instrument which does for the eye what the phonograph does for the ear." The magic lantern was probably one of the most popular instruments ever made. It worked its charms at first on children and was later taken up by families as home entertainment and by the sciences as an educational tool. Millions knew its enchantment.

The lantern shows projected and retrieved fantasy and introduced a vivid new world. They rocked one into dreams that often only money could buy. They were the perfect vehicle for railroad publicity. As the capacity of the magic lantern evolved, its shows produced a form of cinematic illusionism with a tapestry of hand-colored photographic images, projected by a powerful arc light, that rendered a stirring and unforgettable luminosity. The lantern effect was magic. Pure sentience. There was something of the campfire experience in watching these illuminations. Fields of light. Fleeting moments frozen in time and transformed into a permanent record. Aside from theater and photographs, and until the birth of motion pictures in the 1890s, the magic-lantern slide show was the major mass visual medium of its time.

In principle, a magic-lantern show was no more or less magical than a modern slide show.[4] The basic technical ingredients were the same: a source of light, a system of condensers and lenses, an image, and a white or light-colored surface onto which the image was projected. In the magic lantern, the light source evolved from oil lamps to carbon arcs, and then to modern filament lamps.

The sources of the magic-lantern images, however, were quite different from those used in modern projectors. Since World War II, any amateur photographer can generate 35mm color transparencies for the purposes of projection. Creating an image for the magic lantern was not that easy. Before the invention of photography, images were hand-painted and etched on glass by specialists. Those pieces of glass, which came to be known as lantern slides, were conventionalized into a rectangular format measuring 3¼ × 4 inches. By the 1840s, it was possible to apply actual photographic images to the lantern slide. However, the commercial potential of lantern slides could not be fully realized until existing techniques for hand-coloring were used to enhance the black-and-white photographic images.

An important aspect of the challenge of producing a fine hand-colored lantern slide, which may not be immediately apparent, was the scale at which the colorist worked. The watchmaker-like care that was required of the colorist is captured succinctly by a contemporary photographic historian: "Lantern-slide painting was a delicate and painstaking art, for although the slides were no smaller than most miniature work, they were enlarged by hundreds of diameters, and thus the most insignificant flaw was increased to embarrassing proportions."[5]

Once it was possible to produce hand-colored photographic slides, one had ready-made dreams for sale. A large variety of slides was available. In 1891, for example, a London firm advertised that it kept a stock of two million lantern slides.[6] Special lantern catalogues offered a wide choice, covering such subjects as the American Civil War, the Chinese Empire Illustrated, Portraits of Distinguished Americans, Scenes Illustrating James Fenimore Cooper's Novels, American and Foreign Scenery, Views in the Holy Land, and American Historical and Literary Curiosities. Travelogue series enjoyed an especially widespread popularity.[7]

ALBERT EINSTEIN AND HIS WIFE, WITH HOPI INDIANS AT HOPI HOUSE, GRAND CANYON, ARIZONA

An important feature of a magic-lantern show was the novel visual experience it provided. Until the period of cinema, the lantern slide was the only existing medium that allowed large groups of people to see projected images and to be transported figuratively to distant places. People were urged "to indulge in a lantern," "to go in for lantern showings and give pleasure to one's friends and children."[8]

W. H. Simpson, an amateur photographer himself, advocated the promotion of the hand-colored lantern slide as a cozy and imaginative vehicle with which to slip inside the American psyche. The Santa Fe Railway extended the use of this popular and versatile medium from an educational tool, news vehicle, and popular form of entertainment to an agent of tourism. The hand-colored lantern slide was widely circulated as an advertising feature of the railway. It was portable, cheap, effective, and fun.

The advertising department of the Santa Fe used the language of color aggressively and imaginatively. Color was one of its greatest assets. The campaigns to promote travel on the Santa Fe evoked a golden age where color glowed and image flowered. One might say that it possessed the property that Saint Thomas ascribed only to angels when he maintained that one of their characteristics is the ability to leave one place for another without having to move at all! The colorist was a metaphysician of the festive and the ceremonial. He had the power to move us in and out of worlds of irrepressible richness and to shift us from the delightful and wonder-full to the awesome and serious. The image makers understood the immediacy of color, which the black-and-white tradition could not offer, and they used its vividness with great effect to inform, distract, dazzle, captivate, and mesmerize. Color was its own kingdom.

The most extensively used method for mass producing colored photographic images was hand-coloring. By adding color to the monochrome image, the photograph was made that much more real, thereby heightening the perception of the viewer. Until the availability and practicality of modern color photography for the general public in the late 1930s, the strong demand for colored photographs was satisfied by hand-colorists.[9] Many of them were portrait painters and miniaturists, who found themselves out of work as a result of photography. Paradoxically, the public ardor for colored photographs was not shared by artists and photographers. Not a few considered color to be a vulgar aberration, with its "artificial hues" and "unnatural effects" and, accordingly, held it in low esteem. Moreover, many hand-colorists were thought to lack a "clear understanding of the principles of harmonious coloring, of the gradation of colors as seen in natural objects, and in the exercise of restraint and common sense."[10]

Ample and exquisite examples of the "art" of hand-coloring do, however, exist. The Santa Fe lantern shows were melodies of light and color. Some of the most delicately colored and luminous images emerged, such as *Navajo Maiden*, page 152, or *Mirror Lake, Yosemite*, page 84. The tinting achieved by the photographic colorist could be of such subtle softness, warmth, and lifelike appearance that it would be easy to confuse this distinguished work with the best examples of modern color photography. Instances of this fine brushwork are provided by *Indian Girl on Ladder, Hopi*, page 109, and *The Altar Falls, Grand Canyon*, page 65. Such faithful attention to the tinting of landscapes often resulted in the actual enhancement of natural beauty, even though the coloring of sky, water, and rocks may have been idealized, as in *Nevada Falls*, page 79. Subtlety and fine gradation of color might well contribute to the ringing of mood and the breathing of raw intent, as in *Pueblo Potter Mixing Clay*, page 105. The picture rains pathos; a lace of sadness filters through the air of the potter's world. The color elicits an intimate sensation and now and then we may delight in overhearing a vacant thought.

In contrast, crudely painted scenes achieved the sentimental and the slightly ridiculous and rendered a colored postcard effect, as in *Navajo Couple*, page 148, a whimsical look at what might well read as "the old folks at home." A similar example of undisciplined coloring can be seen in *Married and Unmarried Hopi Women* (page 110).

One of the strongest properties of color is the breadth of feeling it can evoke. An impressive example is illustrated by two renditions of identical photographs of Mirror Lake in Yosemite National Park (page 84). The Santa Fe Railway used both versions in the same lantern-show presentation, to obvious advantage. Starting with the same monochrome image, the colorist was able to "take" the same photograph twice. The result is two dramatic and very different effects; in this case, a sense of sunset (or sunrise) and of mid-morning.

Even when color was used poorly, the public was entranced by its charms. Color ornamented, adorned, enlivened. It had the effect of jeweling sadness and wrapping picturesquely intervals of forgotten time. Color infused the lantern images with a unique visual drama. It was exotic and it created mystery. A visual impact of primeval gardens. Color resonated with highly charged associations, like fragments of remembered dreams. "Sunday school colored slides formed our images then," recalled writer Howard Fast. "We had no other really 'live' impressions at that time, so the lantern and color made quite an impact."[11]

DETOURING THE INDIAN

... we Americans, who would travel by the many thousand, if we had the chance, to see a Homeric rite in Attica, or a serpent ceremony in old Egypt, are only beginning to realize that the snake-dance at Walpi, or the corn-dance at Cochiti, are also revelations of primitive art, expressions of that original human impulse toward the creation of beauty. . . .

Harriet Monroe (1920)[1]

The skyscraper will scatter on the winds like thistledown, and the geniune America, the America of New Mexico, will start on its course again. This is an interregnum.

D. H. Lawrence (1924)[2]

The Indian Detour was a novel and colorful travel innovation, designed to give cross-country travelers on the Santa Fe an adventurous and romantic interlude away from the railroad. The Detour was an exceedingly shrewd and compelling odyssey into modern advertising practice. The *Albuquerque Morning Journal* described the Santa Fe Railway's Detour as "one of the most important [developments] . . . in modern railroading in that for the first time in history a transportation system will be operating a rail and bus system in parallel lines over a great part of its territory."[3]

The Detour, which was a joint venture with Fred Harvey, made all of northern and central New Mexico and the Hopi villages and Canyon de Chelly of Arizona readily accessible to the sightseer for the first time. A laudatory editorial in the *Albuquerque Morning Journal* announced that the Santa Fe Railway and Fred Harvey had committed themselves to advertise the Detour on a large scale. They would spend " . . . literally hundreds of thousands of dollars . . . in advertising to make the Southwest known to the rest of the world."[4]

Confidence in the success of so ambitious an undertaking as the Indian Detour derived from the popularity of tourism in the Grand Canyon. In 1924, prior to the inception of the Detour, the Santa Fe Railway transported more than fifty thousand passengers to the rim of the Canyon via its spur line from Williams, Arizona. The vast influx of tourists was then taken on sightseeing trips around the edge of the Canyon in Harvey buses.

The first Indian Detour took place on May 15, 1926. The Detours were advertised and sold by more than twelve thousand travel agents throughout the United States and Europe. They promised an unprecedented and portentous experience for the traveler. The tourist was enticed by advertising copy which proclaimed that "there is more of historic, prehistoric, human and scenic interest in New Mexico than in any other similar area in the world, not excepting India, Egypt, Europe or Asia."[5] Additional promotion was provided by guides of the Indian Detour, who were sent out as emissaries to lecture extensively throughout the United States to Rotary Clubs, church groups, college alumni organizations, and travel bureaus. The guides often illustrated their talks with lantern slides depicting the scenic and native attractions of the Detour. Another way in which guides solicited tourists for the Detour was to sell tickets directly to passengers traveling the Santa Fe's cross-country route. "Once I sold a tour to a party of Japanese," recalled a former guide from Santa Fe. "The Japanese women were dressed in their native costume. It was pretty hard to tell which group was more interested in the other, the Japanese or the Indians."[6]

Hundreds of thousands of people first saw the Southwest and the Indian under the auspices of the Indian Detours. One veteran guide reported that she was personally responsible for as many as ten thousand tourists a year.[7] Some of the distinguished participants of the Detour included Eleanor Roosevelt and her entourage, Harry Guggenheim and family, Albert Einstein and his wife, John D. Rockefeller, Jr., and family, and visiting European royalty.[8]

The Indian Detour was sold as part of the regular ticket on the Santa Fe transcontinental trains. The general plan of the Detour was a "personally conducted" all-expense motor trip, under Santa Fe–Fred Harvey management, covering nearly three hundred miles and lasting two to three days. A three-day trip to Taos Pueblo, for example, cost $65. The idea was not only to bring tourists directly to New Mexico—something

INDIANS GREET RAIL PASSENGERS AT RIM OF GRAND CANYON

which had never been done before on so large a scale—but also to achieve the far more important goal of introducing Easterners to the state's resources, beauties, and Indian pueblos.

Visits to the Indian pueblos of Taos, Tesuque, San Ildefonso, Santa Clara, and Laguna Pueblo, as well as to the prehistoric communal ruins of Tyuonyi and Puye were regularly featured highlights of the Detour. By 1929, a Detour car could be hired, complete with chauffeur and guide, for about $100 a day and one could go anywhere in the Southwest where there was a reasonable trail.[9] At this time, there were no paved roads, no direction signs, and no bridges over arroyos on the scheduled trips of the Detour.

Packard and Cadillac seven-passenger touring cars, the first "road Pullmans" ever, with chauffeurs and "couriers" (the railroad's term for guides) met the "detourists" either at Albuquerque, if they came from the West, or at Las Vegas, New Mexico, if they came from the East. Buses with seating capacities of sixteen to twenty-five persons " . . . having . . . revolving cushioned seat[s] as in parlor cars and . . . built for highest visibility from all sides" were designed especially for the Detour.[10] The Detourists were whisked off the beaten path into the hills that offered Indians, ruins, and artists as equal attractions. After the Detour, the tourist rejoined the railroad to continue his journey.

Tourists were lured to the new exotic theater of the Southwest with promises of comfort and style. The Indian Detour was promoted as a photographic ramble through Indian country for the well-heeled, "the most discriminating traveler" who wished to explore the way of life of "the first Americans." The Detour was an exercise in roughing it—deluxe.

The tourists' manner of arrival was not always compatible with the serious purpose of the occasion:

> One trip greatly enhanced by the new arrangements was the tour to the Hopi Mesas . . . Because there were no accommodations at the villages, the accommodations were loaded on trucks and brought to the site. Large tents complete with cots, blankets, pillows, lanterns and wash basins made portable hotels, not up to the Harvey standards, but this was acceptable to the dudes. Tables and chairs were trucked out to make portable dining halls. Foodstuffs, beverages, cooking equipment, cooling devices, all assured the tourist they would eat unspoiled food, prepared in the Harvey Hotel kitchen, served, if not with candelabra . . . at least with napery. . . . There was even hot tea to bring a touch of grace to the meal. . . . [11]

The event was the Hopi Snake Dance.

Erna Fergusson, who schooled the first Detour couriers, recounted some exotic sights that awaited the willing Detourist: "Motorists crossing the Southwestern States are nearer to the primitive than anywhere else on the continent. They are crossing a land in which a foreign people, with foreign speech and foreign ways, offer them spectacles which can be equaled in a very few Oriental lands."[12] Fergusson urged Easterners to experience "the feather dance in which a feather stands upright in a basket and, untouched and alone, dances in time with a dancing man. Weirder and wilder . . . is the fire dance. Old men sing in their typical, complaining note, while young men, smeared with gray earth, leap and bound through the flames, beating themselves and each other with burning brands, and trilling high mad calls."[13] Similar spectacles were described in the lavish eighty-six-page folders that the Santa Fe printed to promote the distinctive features of the Detour and of its line. Many of the brochures and folders contain images that have an enchanted silence about them. An offer of many serene hours. A world innocent of threatening forces. "Surrounded by fantastic flourishes of gold thread," the folders cast the spell, inviting one into the realm of the primitive and the exoticism of "buried cities." The Santa Fe advertising copy brimmed with the *rhetoric of belonging* that was aimed at an impressionable and nationalistically minded public. With patriotic allure, their Indian Detour advertisements invited the tourist to discover an "unknown" America: "Off the beaten paths in our Far Southwest . . . many are the paths of the Indians, worn inches deep in solid rock by moccasined feet. . . . They lead away into the hinterlands of New Mexico and Arizona, from the familiar beaten path of the railroad. They criss-cross a last frontier that has taken 350 years to subdue. They find out buried cities . . . and string together age-old Indian pueblos where one may 'catch archaeology alive.'"[14]

One of the Detour couriers continued this theme when she spoke publicly of the "magic [that was] hidden in the Southwest for hundreds of years, but is now being opened up for the traveler by the Santa Fe" and of the "motor service [that is] second to none in the world."[15] She concluded that it was "necessary in this little known country to have someone interpret the country as well as take care of all the bothersome details of travel."

As stimulating and informative as the Detours were, the perception of Indian life provided by the railroad was no more or less penetrating than what one would expect from a good "tour operator." There was virtually no hint of poverty or disease in this private diary, nor an awareness of the great violence wreaked by sudden windstorms and devastating flash floods in this naturally disaster-prone environment. The 1920s were characterized by epidemics of measles and dysentery, forced public "dippings" of the Hopi in sheep disinfectants to prevent infestation, and the pervasive and destructive use of alcohol.[16] Problems of overgrazing and severe droughts reduced much of the landscape to a raw and sore condition. It was also a time when native dances were prohibited by the federal government.

JOHN SLOAN, INDIAN DETOUR, *ETCHING, 1927*

The scene was identified as the Corn Dance at Santo Domingo Pueblo and in Sloan's own words is "a satire on the Harvey Indian Tour."[17]

By carefully excluding evidence of the harshness of human existence, the Santa Fe created a romantic and one-dimensional view of Indian life and the Southwest landscape. The railroad's impoverished view of Indian life brings to mind *The Silent Language* of Edward T. Hall: "Culture hides much more than it reveals, and strangely what it hides, it hides most effectively from its own participants."[18]

What the Detours did succeed in creating, however, was a horde of urban consumers. The Indian was promoted as an item to be consumed by the tourist. Mary McCarthy's observation that "the idea of loot is pretty fundamental to the tourist experience" captures succinctly the approach that the Santa Fe used in enticing tourists to buy the "authentic" Indian souvenir.[19] Although Indians did make pottery, jewelry, and religious items, their primary motivation was not commercial. The Santa Fe Railway and the Fred Harvey Company changed this. They began systematically to promote mass production of crafts. In the process, they set up the Indians as skilled commercial artisans. A dramatic shift took place—away from the tradition of Indian vessels as religious and utilitarian objects to an arts-and-crafts industry geared to the parlor tastes of the East. Indian culture was turned into a highly salable commodity that was marketed as pottery, woven blankets, paintings, and baskets. For a fee, songs and dances were also performed for the tourists. Both sides benefited. The new arts-and-crafts industry provided financial assistance to needy native communities and notoriety to some Indian artisans. It brought joy as well as a new awareness of native crafts to collectors of Southwestern art and to tourists and it appealed to American nationalism. Furthermore, the promotion of Indian "artifacts" by Fred Harvey and the Santa Fe Railway enhanced their prestige and business flourished.

In 1914, anthropologist Walter Hough noted that everyone who visited Hopi country brought away, as a souvenir, pottery created by Nampeyo, the famous Hopi potter from the Pueblo of Hano. By 1919, Nampeyo's Hopi bowls were displayed in every Harvey store from New Mexico to California. The railroad manipulated the market through their advertising in order to give Indian artifacts an unprecedented "art" status and thus enhance their price. The Indian potters, in turn, satisfied the demands of the acquisitive tourists. In some instances, artificial "artifacts" were mass produced, such as the *Tesuque Rain God* (page 57), which played no actual role in Indian culture. In fact, they had little connection to anything other than a burgeoning souvenir market. This led very quickly to the production of great quantities of "curios," supervised by the railway and traders to satisfy the growing demands of a flourishing tourist market created by the railway.

With the establishment of the Indian Detour, the Santa Fe advertising department surpassed itself in the promotion of the frontier of Americana—in the folklore of the wilderness and the "primitive." Santa Fe advertising cast the Detour into an "out of this world" setting, heavily veiling it with the haze of quaint exoticism. With their ads extolling a "newly found" culture of a "gentle, peaceful and picturesque people" who lived a "nature-loving" way of life, the Santa Fe admen created the impression that they were the saviors of a lost civilization.

The image makers gave "primitive life" and the "wilderness" respectability. They canvased the varied landscapes for tourist potential, and from strange and exotic vistas they created a thrilling phantasmagoria. In the name of fun and an original experience, "scenic pageantry" was proffered as "our last frontier . . . of . . . picturesque peoples . . . [who] wander the plains with flocks and herds." One was invited to "feel the epic of America . . . [and to] know what is left of primitive America," away from the growing anarchy of the skyscraper. [20]

The Santa Fe's success hinged upon its sensitivity to the public's prototype of the Indian. The railroad's highly polished and compelling images of Indian "reality" came to supersede reality itself, and the Indian was called into synthetic being. This was accomplished by isolating him from his own environment and putting him on display as a social object. Nevertheless, the entire advertising enterprise galvanized a public into a new awareness of the diversity and richness within their own country.

With the success of the Santa Fe's rhetoric of belonging, culture and land were appropriated. In annexing the history of a land and the experience and wisdom of a people for corporate self-enhancement, the railroad inevitably arrogated truth exclusively to itself. The wonders they presented to the world, however, would become commonplace in tourist advertising. But before that would happen, the shape and the techniques of American "corporate poetry"—the song of Southwest Indian life and blooming desert heartlands—reached out and touched the hearts of countless individuals.

MEN TRAVEL WIDELY TO DIFFERENT SORTS OF PLACES SEEKING DIF-
FERENT DISTRACTIONS BECAUSE THEY ARE FICKLE . . . AND ALWAYS
SEEK AFTER SOMETHING WHICH ELUDES THEM.

SENECA (ROMAN ESSAYIST)[1]

HOW SAD THE FLESH! AND THERE'S
NO MORE TO READ.
ESCAPE, FAR OFF! . . .
I SHALL DEPART! STEAMER WITH SWAYING MASTS,
RAISE ANCHOR FOR EXOTIC WILDERNESS!

STÉPHANE MALLARMÉ, "BRISE MARINE"[2]

WHEN YOU GET THERE, THERE ISN'T ANY THERE THERE.

GERTRUDE STEIN[3]

ANYONE CONCERNED WITH THE MOTIVATION OF TRAVEL HAS TO RE-
ALISE FIRST THAT HE IS REACHING DEEP INTO ONE OF THE MAJOR
CONFLICTS OF THE HUMAN MIND: A DESIRE FOR SAMENESS, THE RE-
TURN TO THE WOMB, IF YOU WISH; CONFLICTING WITH THE MOTIVA-
TION TO REACH OUT AND DISCOVER THE WORLD. IN A SUBLIMATED
FASHION, A TRIP IS THEREFORE A FORM OF BIRTH OR REBIRTH.

DR. ERNEST DICHTER[4]

ROUGHING IT IN STYLE

IN SEARCH OF THE SIMPLE AND THE EXOTIC

"Eastward I go only by force; but westward I go free. The future lies that way to me . . . I must walk toward Oregon, and not toward Europe." [4a]

By the end of the nineteenth century, many of the characteristics of modern tourism were discernible, but developments in the beginning of this century—notably the completion of extensive railway systems and the introduction of the automobile—added considerably to the volume of traffic and created a new Age of Tourism.

"America was promises," wrote Archibald MacLeish, and the West was a jumping-off point, a fable waiting to be told. It was still a new frontier in the minds of many who sought new vistas and quick fortunes.[5] The Santa Fe Railway explored the possibilities and poetic uses of the wilderness for tourism and corporate self-enhancement and set out to show something different.

The West unfolded with the Santa Fe. It waved, beckoned hypnotically. It fulfilled a longing for adventure and discovery; it offered a respite from the weariness brought on by the anonymity of city life. Santa Fe advertising promised a holiday excursion into the excitements of flight and pursuit—and offered a rebirth of spirit. It proffered a new world, simple and exotic, in the labyrinthine corridors of the wilderness of the American West—the "wondering delight, stupendous formations and strange sublimity" of the Grand Canyon, "bewitching Yosemite," and the "wild joy and ecstasy of the mountains in the distant West." An entire nation was stimulated to visit these "unexplored" regions of the country. Indian culture was still a remote outpost in the Southwest, and the image makers of the Santa Fe invited the tourist to "discover" the "real aboriginal stock of America . . . in all their picturesque life and customs."[6]

Intent upon transplanting Eastern pleasures to the wilderness of the West, the Santa Fe provided "intimate motor cruises" to the prehistoric ruins and Indian pueblos of New Mexico and Arizona. Elaborate picnic hampers and a full tea service were features of these "Indian Detours." Buggy riding along the rim of the Grand Canyon in dancing shoes and ball dresses and mule rides in ornamental riding habits, deep into this great gap of the earth's crust, led one English visitor to the West to remark that "all this seems odd among the mountains."

The swell of fantasy was taken to heart, and tourism in the American Southwest—under the aegis of the Santa Fe Railway—became the new religion. "We shall, like the Athenians of old, 'delicately march in pellucid air,' " wrote a New Englander traveling by rail in the 1890s. "We must cross deserts and scale mountains till we reach the Eden of the West and tread the Hall of Montezuma."[7]

*THE SAGUAROS [CACTUSES]—THEY ARE INDIANS TOO. YOU DON'T
<u>EVER</u> THROW <u>ANYTHING</u> AT THEM. IF YOU HIT THEM IN THE HEAD
WITH ROCKS YOU COULD KILL THEM. YOU DON'T EVER STICK ANY-
THING SHARP INTO THEIR SKIN, EITHER, OR THEY WILL JUST DRY
UP AND DIE. YOU DON'T DO ANYTHING TO HURT THEM. THEY <u>ARE</u>
INDIANS.*

PAPAGO INDIAN[8]

THE WONDER BUS AND TRAILER IN SAGUARO NATIONAL MONUMENT, NEAR PAPAGO INDIAN RESERVATION, ARIZONA

Travelers passing the Pueblo villages of the Southwest in the 1890s were invited to recall the villages of ancient Egypt, Nubia, and Babylon, rather than to study the remnants of American aboriginal life, observed one historian.[9] But by the beginning of this century, when the Santa Fe Railway began to feature Indians in its advertising of the Southwest, the Indian had achieved a negotiable value as decoration. The Santa Fe began to run sight-seeing trips via its spurs and short lines through northern and southern Arizona to the Painted and Sonora deserts. The Papago Indians ("Desert People") lived fifty miles southwest of Tucson.

The Papago view the saguaro cactus not as a separate life form but very much as a part of mankind. These spectacular giants grow to a height of nearly fifty feet and have a life span of from one hundred and fifty to two hundred years. They provide the fruit pulp from which one of the few native alcoholic beverages is made—a vital life-giving force for all Papago Indians.

"THIS COUNTRY DOESN'T SEEM TO BE INHABITED."
"NO ONE LIVES NEAR HERE," THE COURIER ADMITTED.
"WELL, THEN!" THE WOMAN EXCLAIMED, "AREN'T YOU AFRAID OF BANDITS?"
"WHAT DO YOU MEAN?" ASKED THE COURIER.
"BANDITS!" FIERCELY CAME THE REPLY. "WILD MEN. ISN'T THIS MEXICO?"

FRED HARVEY COMPANY
TOURIST AT FRIJOLES CANYON,
NEW MEXICO[10]

VOLCANIC ROCKS. CUMBRES PASS, NEW MEXICO

On May 15, 1926, a bold new experiment in touring, the Indian Detour, was launched by the Santa Fe Railway and the Fred Harvey Company. A fleet of Packard automobiles, the first "road Pullmans" ever, whisked a few privileged tourists off the beaten path to the Indian pueblos and ruins of New Mexico and Arizona. The cars were painted "Tesuque" brown and displayed a stylized version of the Indian Thunderbird as an official insignia on the door. Tourists were called "detourists" or "dudes," their guides were "couriers," and the drivers, "navigators." The Detour created a unique tourist environment. The cars were the very model of luxury, with heavy leather upholstery, folding rear-seat windshields, and two jump seats. Billed as a "land-cruise" for the "most discriminating traveler," the motor trip deluxe focused on the "re-discovery of America" through the "Original Americans." Tourists were invited to camp out in style with the Indians.

CRYSTAL TRADING POST—GENERAL VIEW—CRYSTAL, NEW MEXICO

Crystal, near the Arizona–New Mexico border, was a favorite base of photographers and tourists for expeditions to the pueblos and the Navajo country of Canyon de Chelly. It was also the place where the highly prized Navajo rug was made. Buyers from all over came to purchase the "crystal style" rug, whose design was greatly influenced by businessman and promoter J.B. Moore. When Moore bought the Crystal Trading Post in 1897, he found the workmanship of Navajo weaving to be careless and loose. With promotional flare, he recognized the potential of the Navajo blanket as a major economic commodity. At once he suggested particular designs and colors he knew would appeal to the tastes of urban buyers. A popular example, distinguished by interlocking diamonds, border designs, and later by Oriental motifs, became known as the "crystal style." The Navajos were quick to adapt to the new market demands. Moore also encouraged an adaptation of the Navajo classic design. With these new developments, the 1890s witnessed the end of the traditional Navajo blanket as a native item of personal use (the Navajos wore machine-made products thereafter) and ushered in a highly productive era of rugs-for-trade. A valuable commodity was introduced, but the blanket as an expression of the manifestation of the soul-spirit disappeared.

TONTO TRAIL, NEAR HORN CREEK, GRAND CANYON

"There are mules and horses for the trails that would fill a ranchman's corral," reported a seasoned traveler to the Grand Canyon in 1917, "while, beyond the station, there are miles of sidings where long trains of solid Pullmans, four, five or six sections to one schedule, each one with two engines, are equipped to haul two thousand persons in or out per day. This resort has 'arrived.' And there arrive here daily and stay weekly, monthly, notables from all four quarters of the habitable earth." In his Going Abroad Overland: Studies of Places and People in the Far West, *David M. Steele continues his description of his first encounter with the Titan of Chasms: "The first and possibly the most astonishing thing the traveler to Grand Canyon experiences is the fortunate nature of the approach to it. There is absolutely nothing to apprise you that the place is nearer than a million miles until you step out of the train right at its edge, almost right into it. A hole more than a mile deep at the side door of a railway station and hotel which you have entered from an absolutely level course across the desert . . . The train . . . comes to a sudden stop. And you are at the gate of Heaven."[11]*

NEW MEXICO HAD BEEN DISCOVERED BY ARTISTS [AND TOURISTS BY THE 1920S]. IN A FRENETIC EFFORT TO ESCAPE THE COMPLICATIONS OF WESTERN CITIES, THEY WERE SEEKING NOT ONLY THE PEACE OF THE DESERT, BUT THE REFRESHMENT OF PRIMITIVE LIFE....JADED AND NERVE-WRACKED AESTHETES PLUNGED INTO IT....NOTHING WAS TOO EXTREME TO EXPRESS THEIR DESIRE TO GO WESTERN, INDIAN, TO LIVE SIMPLY.... EVERYBODY HAD A PET PUEBLO, A PET INDIAN, A PET CRAFT. PET INDIANS WITH POTTERY, BASKETS, AND WEAVING TO SELL WERE SEATED BY THE CORNER FIREPLACE (COPIED FROM THE PUEBLO), PLIED WITH TOBACCO AND COFFEE, ASKED TO SING AND TELL TALES....WITTER BYNNER BOUGHT AND WORE AND HUNG ON HIS FRIENDS A FAMOUS COLLECTION OF INDIAN JEWELRY. ALICE CORBIN INTRODUCED THE VELVET NAVAHO BLOUSE. STETSON HATS, COWBOY BOOTS, FLANNEL SHIRTS, EVEN BLANKETS WERE THE AP-PROVED COSTUME....MARY AUSTEN DISCOVERED AND ORDERED HER LIFE TO THE BEAT OF THE AMERINDIAN RHYTHM....
IT WAS OBLIGATORY TO GO TO EVERY PUEBLO DANCE. FAILURE TO APPEAR ON A SUNNY ROOF ON EVERY SAINT'S DAY MARKED ONE AS SOULLESS AND WITHOUT TASTE.

ERNA FERGUSSON
(AUTHOR AND INSTRUCTOR OF
FRED HARVEY COMPANY COURIERS)[12]

"GOLD TOOTH JOHN," JICARILLA APACHE CHIEF AT TAOS PUEBLO, NEW MEXICO

The rugged peaks of the spectacular Sangre de Cristo (Blood of Christ) range form a dramatic backdrop for the life of the Tiwa people. With the summer suns, the snowcapped peaks melt and pure streams come tumbling down to the mesa areas below, irrigating many fertile valleys.

Annual trips into the Plains country were made by some of the northern Rio Grande Pueblo Indians "to camp, visit and hunt buffalo with the Comanches," notes native anthropologist Edward Dozier. As recently as the thirties, observes Dozier, the old men "spoke with nostalgia of these sojourns into the Plains country, [but] the destruction of the buffalo and the placement of the Plains Indians on reservations ended these contacts."[13] What this Apache was doing at Taos we cannot know; he was perhaps visiting on the pueblo's saint's day. Inter-town visiting and trading were considerable among Pueblo Indians. Other reasons for visiting might include participation in an initiation rite and competitive inter-pueblo games, such as the popular foot races.

PREHISTORIC CAVE DWELLINGS. FRIJOLES CANYON, BANDELIER NATIONAL MONUMENT, NEW MEXICO

In 1890, the explorer Adolph Bandelier described his discovery of Frijoles Canyon as "the grandest thing I ever saw." His diary entry records his "... almost precipitous descent into the Canyon.... The cliffs are vertical on the north side, and their bases are ... used as dwellings.... There are some of one, two and three stories.... The plaster is still in the rooms. Some are walled in; others are mere holes in the rocks. Much pottery ... I found entire chimneys, metates, manos, and a stone-axe."[14] Established as a national monument in 1916, Bandelier is located on the Pajarito Plateau in the canyon and mesa country of northern New Mexico, twenty miles from Santa Fe. It is a region containing many remarkable prehistoric ruins. Cliff houses and conical cave rooms extend for two miles along the north wall of the canyon. "Villages" were built out of the slopes of talus (accumulated rock and dirt) at the bases of the cliffs, and "houses" were fashioned from the steep precipices of tuff (layers of comparatively soft, compacted volcanic ash).

TESUQUE WOMAN MAKING RAIN GODS

Traditionally, vessels in human and animal form made by the Tewa at the pueblo of Tesuque had religious and utilitarian purposes. The function of these vessels was altered when the railroad began enticing tourists (in the early 1900s) to "travel the Santa Fe all the way" to the Southwest. Together with the Fred Harvey Company, the Santa Fe created a tourist-oriented arts-and-crafts industry where none had existed previously. Indian artisans were put on display in the Indian Room, a novel attraction of the Alvarado Hotel in Albuquerque, built in 1902 by the Santa Fe and Fred Harvey. Here, tourists could observe "patient Navajo squaws weaving blankets" and "Indians from Acoma and Laguna making pottery." They could buy these appealing items, and many more, in the curio shop next door. An inevitable by-product of the merchandising of Indian culture was the production of great quantities of "curios" like the Tesuque Rain God.[15]

GEOGRAPHY COMES TO AN END,
COMPASS HAS LOST ALL EARTHLY NORTH,
HORIZONS HAVE NO MEANING,
NOR ROADS AN EXPLANATION.
                    THOMAS MERTON
                    (AMERICAN POET
                    AND PHILOSOPHER)[16]

"INTEREST QUICKENS," ROWE'S POINT, GRAND CANYON

The Grand Canyon is one of the strangest and most spectacular wonders of the earth. It is a stunning tapestry of sustained, stratified brilliance. The sheets of color are endless, radiating a nacreous kind of beauty. Silence is in them, arresting thought. It is a breathless moment, the first viewing, and the soul whirls as it encounters a divinity of cathedral lightness.

The canyon is ancient as antiquity, yet not old. Beyond the rim, one looks back to a time when the earth was young, nearly two billion years ago. But the canyon's formation took somewhere between six and thirty million years, a mere breath of geologic time. More than two thousand prehistoric Indian sites speckle the canyon, and numerous nineteenth-century mining camps still remain, crumpled reminders of silvered hopes, ineffable defeats, and a few hard-won rewards.

GRAND CANYON

A Chinese guidebook to a famous mountain states that "unless a mountain has strange peaks and curious rocks to shape its scenic beauty . . . it will not claim the attention of generations of people." At the Grand Canyon, unearthly space and silence confront and encapsulate. The canyon prompts affinities to the primordial, colored, Oriental. The buttes and mesas loom imaginatively. Improbability dominates—exerting an irresistible appeal, a hermetic romanticism, a respect for the unknowable. Time ceases to exist and the resonating, luminous shapes cast their strange and penetrating reflections upon the soul of the abyss with a delicacy and grace unique. It is an example of the pellucidity of light, unharnessed, catching flame.

GRAND CANYON VISTA, AT GRAND VIEW POINT

In 1901 the Santa Fe Railway introduced a new age of tourism with the completion of its spur line from Williams, Arizona, to the south rim of the canyon. With the construction there in 1905 of a unique resort-hotel complex, the El Tovar, the canyon became the place to vacation. For the first time, it became accessible to the urban hordes rather than to the select hardy few who had previously braved the rigors of coach and wagon travel to the brink of the gorge. The hotel was a great lure of tourist traffic, promising all the comforts of home. In 1920 writer and traveler John C. van Dyke commented on its influence upon the "new tourist." "The hotel is far too beguiling. From that comfortable quarter you look out and perhaps indolently come to the conclusion that you are seeing the whole Canyon. Nine out of ten rest content with that view and that conclusion. They get no farther than the benches along the Rim. . . . When the evening train goes out they go with it, rather glad that they came, and quite satisfied perhaps that they have 'seen' the Canyon."[17]

*THIS IS MY HEART AS I TRAVEL ALL OVER; MY SPIRIT, MY LIFE AND
LIVING.*

FLATHEAD INDIAN TRAVELING SONG[18]

GRAND CANYON VISTA

"Vacationing has ceased to be aristocratic and exclusive," observed a Californian in 1929, and "it has become more and more difficult to find an exclusive place in which to practice it."[19]

THE OLD PROSPECTOR

This weathered canyon recluse was one of the first to guide tourists down into the Grand Canyon with his pack burros. He came to the canyon in the early 1880s to hunt and prospect but found a better living as a guide. A distinguished traveler recorded his enthusiastic impressions of such a character after seeing the canyon in the early days of this century: "[He was] a genius, a philosopher and a poet, the possessor of a fund of information vastly important, if true. He laughs with the giddy, yarns to the gullible, talks sense to the sedate, and is a most excellent judge of scenery, human nature and pie. To see the Canyon only, and not to see [such a character] is to miss half the show."[20]

CAMPSITE. THE ALTAR FALLS (OR RIBBON FALLS), BRIGHT ANGEL CREEK, GRAND CANYON

It was not uncommon to see campers in wilderness areas at the turn of the century. Many came with their families, some with wagons, and some even with a Chinese cook! A word of advice for the prospective camper in 1905 was offered by Mrs. Ernest Thompson Seton. (She was married to the artist, writer, and famous naturalist Ernest Seton. Together they established, in 1930, Seton Village, a twenty-five-hundred-acre community dedicated to the study of nature and the promotion of recreation and the outdoor arts.) Mrs. Seton advised: "Dear woman who goes hunting with her husband, be sure that you have it understood that you do no cooking or dishwashing. . . . See that for your camping trip [there] is provided a man cook!"[21]

THE DIAMOND HITCH, GRAND CANYON

A mysterious and little-known rope-tying technique was often used when pack mules or other animals carried loads of tourists' provisions into the Grand Canyon. It was called a "diamond hitch." "Throwing the diamond hitch" is an expression frequently encountered in Western literature, but few know anything about it except those who have used it. An ordinary knot is tied, but a diamond hitch is thrown. It is made from a rope forty to fifty feet in length. One end is tied to a pack harnass and the other, or "running part," is thrown back and forth across the animal until the distinctive diamond shape is fashioned and the load is secured.[22]

HERMIT CAMPS

Hermit shale is exemplary of the rock that forms the cliffwork and sculpture of the Grand Canyon. The erosion and weathering of these rocks have produced amazing shapes and horizontal bands of rainbow colors that flood the canyon with crimson and gold. The canyon never ceases to glow with strange and unearthly forms.

PARTY OUTSIDE DINING HALL, PHANTOM RANCH, GRAND CANYON

Phantom Ranch lies some five thousand feet below the rim of the canyon. It offers the traveler rustic surroundings in a retreat of petrified silence, encircled by countless domes and hanging canyons. Designed by architect Mary Jane Colter and completed in 1922, the central lodge features a large swimming pool filled with crystal-clear water. The route of the five-and-a-half-hour mule trip down to the ranch follows the desolate cliffs of the inner gorge, crosses a 420-foot suspension bridge over the Colorado River, and winds its way up Bright Angel Canyon to a small green oasis nestled among the towering crags of a hollow, uptilted world.[23]

THE GRAND CANYON, VIEW FROM TONTO PLATEAU

This view of the world's deepest canyon was taken from within the canyon's inner gorge. In the foreground, the dominant dark rock is the Vishnu schist, a lavalike formation. It is the lowest layer within the canyon and also the oldest—thought to have been formed some two billion years ago. The metamorphic rock, which was formed under great heat and pressure, creates a landscape of charred language. Cutting through this gorge is the Colorado River. In 1869 Major John Powell, a geologist and one-armed veteran of the Civil War known as the first person to descend the Grand Canyon and its mighty Colorado, entered into his journal of August 21: "From around this curve there came a mad roar, and down we are carried with a dizzying velocity to the head of another rapid . . . we have a wild, exhilarating ride for ten miles, which we make in less than an hour. The excitement is so great that we forget the danger until we hear the roar of a great fall below. . . ." [24]

THE BOX CANYON ON BRIGHT ANGEL CREEK, GRAND CANYON

In 1892, the Santa Fe Railway provided the famous painter Thomas Moran with transportation to the Grand Canyon. In return, the artist agreed to relinquish the copyright to Grand Canyon, *the spectacular canvas he painted for the railroad. Moran traveled by rail as far as Flagstaff, Arizona, and from there proceeded by stagecoach to the south rim of the canyon. He described his first viewing of the great chasm in a letter to his wife, Mary: "After dinner (flour cake and bacon) we struck out for the Cañon. On reaching the brink the whole gorge for miles lay beneath and it was by far the most awfully grand and impressive scene that I have ever yet seen. We had reached the Cañon on the second level or edge of the great gulf. Above and around us rose a wall 2,000 feet and below us a vast chasm 2,500 feet in perpendicular depth and a half mile wide. . . . A suppressed sort of roar [of the Colorado River] comes up constantly from the chasm but with that exception every thing impresses you with an awful stillness."[25]*

WHAT HAVE WE LOST, IN THE WEST?
WE WHO HAVE GONE WEST?
THERE IS NO ANSWER...
AN INDIAN, WALKING WRAPT IN HIS WINDING SHEET
ANSWERS THE QUESTION AS HE PUTS IT, IN HIS STRIDE.

D. H. LAWRENCE (1926)[26]

THE CUSTOMS AND COSTUMES OF THE INDIAN TRIBES GROW MORE
INTERESTING AS OUR ACQUAINTANCE WITH THEM BECOMES LESS
FAMILIAR. IN A WORD, WHAT CEASES TO BE COMMON BEGINS TO BE
VALUED.

WESTERN TRAVELER (1880s)[27]

THE OLD CHIEF, INDIAN WITH POPULAR PLAINS-STYLE DRESS

The photograph is representative of the prevailing turn-of-the-century popular and romantic view of the Indian as mystic warrior of the Plains—an image calculated to appeal to preconceived notions of Indian life as well as to the curious but naive tourist. It was an image that the Santa Fe Railway promoted heavily.

It is not known whether this elder belonged to a Pueblo or a Plains group, though he is dressed in the style of the latter.

Constant contact through the centuries has resulted in the borrowing of customs by both the Pueblo and Plains Indians. Both perform animal and war dances, and each has freely and reciprocally appropriated the other's songs, manners, and customs, out of respect and friendship, and often in a spirit of merriment.

"The Old Chief" could well have been a participant in a Rio Grande pueblo Comanche Dance, which was performed to emulate the spirit of the aggressive and fierce Comanche and to celebrate the Plains horse culture.

PETRIFIED FOREST, RAINBOW FOREST AREA, ARIZONA

At Rainbow Forest, you can take a stroll of more than a thousand years into the past, in a prehistoric forest where trees once grew grand but now have been turned to stone by the unending cycles of erosion and corrosion. Countless specimens of petrified logs are scattered over the innumerable knolls and gulches of the desert plain. Crystals of every sort line the cavities of many of these recumbent trunks: amethyst, topaz, quartz, onyx. They are a sleeping world of glasslike rock. A mosaic of gem-studded iridescence. Chips, chunks, clumps, mother-of-pearl gilt, glisten and illumine the desert pavement. Larger deposits dot the range, varying in size from ten feet to two hundred and fifty feet, dormant "trees of prismatic agate," silent witnesses of the earth's genesis. The ancient forest is also the site of more than three hundred Indian ruins, ranging in size from one-room shelters to a seventy-five-room pueblo. The Santa Fe Railway stops at Adamana, the doorway to this "Valley of the Rocks," a glowing jewel in the Arizona wilderness.

PETRIFIED FOREST, ARIZONA

These conical hills, or "tepees," as they are commonly called, drape their velvet, mineralized folds over the desert floor. They are typical of the erosional formations to be found in the Painted Desert region of Arizona. The startling, dark-red bands represent sedimentary layers of siltstones colored by the presence of iron oxides. The darker layers reveal a high carbon content, while the distinct white bands at the bases of these environmental sculptures display deposits of sandstone.

MR. HERB DUNTON AND MODEL IN FIELD

W. Herbert (Buck) Dunton was one of the founders of the Taos Society of Artists, and like so many artists and writers who decided to settle in New Mexico in the early part of this century, he found the region rich in texture and exoticism and still a virgin source for exciting new visual material. The fundamental character of the land, with its primitivism and blend of Hispanic and Indian cultures, served as a magnetic force that was felt by everyone who visited the region. In 1912 Dunton moved to Taos, where he continued to sketch and illustrate for Harper's, Scribner's, and other popular magazines; he also began to devote much of his time to serious painting. The open range, cowboys, and the Indian "untouched by civilization" were his favorite themes. Dunton was a Westerner at heart; he traveled by horseback and carried a rifle. Reminiscing about this period, he wrote: "The west has passed—more's the pity. In another twenty-five years, the old-time westerner will have gone too—gone with the buffalo and the antelope. I'm going to hand down to posterity a bit of the unadulterated real thing. . . ."[28]

BIG SQUAW BUTTE, KINGMAN, ARIZONA

In the foreground are the exotic Joshua trees, desert monarchs of a vast region of stark desolation. In order to see them one must climb to an elevation of at least three thousand feet. The Joshua tree is a giant yucca, which often attains a height of forty feet. When it blooms in early spring, its branch tips bear clusters of glorious, creamy-white blossoms. In their "selling" of the Southwest, the Santa Fe's business was the cultivation of the wilderness, but those seeking reassurance found it in the irresistible lures presented by other promoters. One historian reports that land promoters "bought barrels of oranges, shipped them out to the desert and attached them to Joshua trees just before the prospective buyers showed up over the horizon. 'Look,' said the promoters, 'if this is the way oranges will grow without irrigation, you can just imagine what they'll do when we get water onto this tract!'"[29]

OCOTILLO PLANTS, DESERT COUNTRY OF NEW MEXICO

The ocotillo (Fouquieria splendens) blooms in the desert during the rainy season and grows to a height of from six to twenty-five feet. These plants are easily recognized by their ten-foot wands, which burst into bloom with torch-like clusters of brilliant scarlet flowers, to which the name "ocotillo" (the Spanish word for "little torch") refers. With their vase-shaped bodies, the ocotillos often resemble loose bundles of dead, dry, whiplike sticks. From time to time, the ocotillo plant puts out small oval leaves, which soon fall off, leaving thorny branches behind.

Obviously, the true color of these plants was lost on the artist who hand-colored this lantern slide.

EAGLE ROCK, PETRIFIED FOREST, ARIZONA

Eagle Rock was so called because eagles once nested on its precarious top, in the midst of Jasper Forest. However, as wind and water continued to beat away at the landscape, familiar features disappeared, stripping the forest of its well-known landmarks. In January, 1941, erosion caused Eagle Rock to crash down. Since then, other spirals have "sprouted up" in its place. The erosion cycle produces new formations each year and exposes more petrified wood and other fossils after nearly two hundred million years of burial. The flat, rocky surface in the foreground is made up of petrified-wood fragments, pebbles, and cobbles, and is known as "desert pavement."

"OSTRICH TREE," A CALIFORNIA CYPRESS

In its promotion of travel to California the Santa Fe Railway promised "every mile a scenic thrill," which included such "picturesque surprises" as the exotic California cypress. "Each tree has its exalted power to bear," wrote Willa Cather of the Southwest landscape.[30] The trees stood at considerable distance from each other, bowing to the breezes with inexorable reserve. "Trees offered man the measure of his upright space . . . they grazed the sky and sounded the underworld . . . their roots went deeper than any creature. . . . From them was born the idea of the pillar, the column."[31]

HALF DOME FROM GLACIER POINT, YOSEMITE

Santa Fe advertising of the "Far West" proffered a magic carpet "away from it all," featuring the "ocean of wilderness and loveliness" of "astonishing Yosemite." Upon viewing Yosemite for the first time in 1863, Frederick Law Olmsted, the noted landscape architect, was overcome by the "union of the deepest sublimity and with the deepest beauty of nature," which made "Yo Semite the greatest glory of nature."[32] Eight years later, the essayist and poet Ralph Waldo Emerson recorded in his journal: "In Yosemite, grandeur of these mountains perhaps unmatched in the globe; for here they strip themselves like athletes for exhibition . . . ."[33]

NEVADA FALLS, YOSEMITE VALLEY, CALIFORNIA

The spectacle of a magnificent waterfall was captured eloquently by Herman Melville: "But perhaps there was nothing about the scenery I beheld more impressive than those silent cascades, whose slender threads of water, after leaping down the steep cliffs, were lost amidst the rich herbage of the valley. Over all the landscape there reigned the most hushed repose, which I almost feared to break, lest, like the enchanted gardens in the fairy tale, a single syllable might dissolve the spell. For a long time, forgetful alike of my own situation, and the vicinity of my still slumbering companion, I remained gazing around me, hardly able to comprehend by what means I had thus suddenly been made a spectator of such a scene."[34]

ON PROSPECT, SHOWING LONGS AND MEEKER

"Dante would have reveled here;

Rembrandt would have gloried

in the mystic shades."[35]

Longs Peak, towering over fourteen thousand feet, is the highest summit in northern Colorado, seventy miles from Denver, and is one of the world's most popular climbs. The Colorado Rockies prompted comparisons by the gentlemen tourists of the 1880s and 1890s to the Swiss Alps: " . . . so surrounded are you by snowy summits that you can easily forget you are in Colorado!"[36] Santa Fe advertising of travel to Colorado emphasized the patriotic. The state was promoted as a new "wealth of wilderness and minerals" no longer "a green and a brown patch of uncertain outlines." Rather it "now . . . lies before us as distinctly as New England and in everything that tends to patriotic ambition, far more attractive."[37]

MIRROR LAKE, YOSEMITE

At the turn of the century, the conventional reply to the objection that "California lacked historical scenery," writes one historian, "was not that it had missions but that it had natural scenery."[38] Magazine reports of visits to Yosemite by distinguished travelers continued to capture the American imagination. One was invited to "worship with Nature" where "you will be mostly in Eternity."[39] Others revealed a journey into "the vale [of] giant domes and battlements."[40] And Walt Whitman insisted on a "feeding visit" in the West for he "wanted new words in writing about these plains and all the inland American West; the terms far, large, vast, etc., are insufficient."[41]

LAKE ELLERY, TIOGA PASS, YOSEMITE NATIONAL PARK

Yosemite Valley was America's first protected natural area. Frederick Law Olmsted was the driving force behind the innovative congressional bill, signed by President Lincoln on June 29, 1864, that established the park as a historic, scenic reserve "for public use, resort and recreation," to be conserved for the State of California, and by implication, for the nation.[42] But travel to Yosemite became famous for its perils and privations. Olmsted reported that tourists arrived "in the majority of cases quite overcome with the fatigue and unaccustomed hardship of the journey. Few persons, especially few women, are able to enjoy or profit by the scenery and air for days afterward . . . many leave before they have recovered from their first exhaustion and return home jaded and ill."[43] It was, declared another distinguished visitor in 1894, the "most exhausting, expensive, and impressive excursion which the tourist can make. . . ."[44] By the close of the century, a writer in Out West noted that travel to Yosemite was "confined almost entirely to the bohemian element and the devotees of science."[45]

THE SIERRA NEVADA RANGE FROM GLACIER POINT, YOSEMITE, CALIFORNIA

In the beginning of this century, the photographer personified the modern hero in cliff-hangers such as this one. He was a conquistador in quest of little-known natural phenomena. His "discoveries" expressed the shock of the new, as well as the spirit of the time. Such a view as this "peeled away the dry wrappers of habitual seeing" and created "another habit of seeing."[46] It breathed sustained danger, projecting the individual right out into the abyss. People at the time had never seen anything quite like it. The daring of it all. It shrieked of adventure and created a powerful stir. Readers of the popular press were invited to join "our photographer" on a journey to the new realms of "the world from above," "the unseen universe," "the miracle of light," and last but not least, "the beauties of every day."[47]

YOSEMITE, CALIFORNIA

In wooing settlers to the West and promoting tourism, the Santa Fe Railway nourished dreams of fertile Edens, a Golden Age where color glowed and image flowered. In this task, the railroad was greatly aided by the rhetoric of nature so widely practiced by leading figures of the time, such as "poet and man of science" John Muir. Muir was "crazy about trees and wild scenes" and was called "mountain-drunk . . . [with] a far-away look in his face and eyes as if he saw the heights and peaks beckoning to him."[48]

YOSEMITE, CALIFORNIA

The Santa Fe Railway advertising department excelled in its reuse of images by hand-coloring copies of the same monochrome photograph quite differently, as can be seen in these identical pictures of Mirror Lake. Hand-colorists learned how to charm the public through various devices; for example, adding "white fleecy clouds, or even a moon" to create different effects.

THREE BROTHERS, YOSEMITE VALLEY

The Sierra Club was established in 1892 under the leadership of John Muir, author, prophet, and conservationist. The club was devoted to the preservation of the American wilderness and the establishment of national parks. Muir was one of the keenest propagators of the national park idea and his book Our National Parks *spread the fame of these parks far and wide. In 1903 Muir and President Theodore Roosevelt disappeared into the woods of the Yosemite Valley for a weekend. It was Roosevelt's first trip to the Far West, and Muir thought he "might be able to do some forest good in freely talking around the campfire."[49] It is thought that a good deal of Roosevelt's conservation policy was formulated then, based on the counsel that John Muir gave the President, who was "not building this country of ours for a day," but "to last through the ages." Muir showed a deep devotion to the Sierra Nevada range. His enthusiasm is epitomized in a letter to Ralph Waldo Emerson, inviting the poet to Yosemite for "a month's worship with Nature in the high temples of the great Sierra Crown beyond our holy Yosemite . . . [where] you will be mostly in Eternity."[50]*

*YOU ASKED ABOUT THE LINE THAT GOES TO THE HEART. IT LEADS
TO THE SPIRIT WHICH RESIDES IN ALL THINGS—THE SPIRIT OF LIFE
AND HOPE. WHEN WE SHOW RESPECT FOR THE SPIRITS AROUND US,
THEY RESPECT US. FROM THIS COMES GOOD. WE SHOW RESPECT IN
PRAYER AND CEREMONY—IN ALL THINGS. WE DEMONSTRATE THIS
BY SHOWING THAT ALL ANIMALS, EVEN SNAKES, POSSESS SOULS.*

HOPI ARTIST[1]

THE HOPI

"When a stranger comes to the village, feed him. Do not injure one another . . . When people are old . . . do not turn

them out . . . [D]o not go out seeking war. The Hopis shall make [this] the Hopi Way."[1a]

The Hopi regard themselves as the first inhabitants of America. Their village of Old Oraibi is considered the oldest and most continuously occupied settlement in North America. The Hopi live in terraced, stone-built villages perched on three mesa tops poised in space between earth and sky in the remote highlands of northern Arizona, one hundred miles east of the Grand Canyon and approximately sixty miles north of the main line of the Santa Fe Railway. Their villages appear to be a continuation of the rock cliffs on which they are built. There is a sense of the ancient here; a timeless serenity envelops this place, suggesting an otherworldliness. Its remoteness establishes an air of mystery. The Hopi call themselves *Hopitu-Shinumu*, best translated as "all people peaceful" or "little people of peace."

There are three villages on First Mesa—Walpi, Sichimovi, and Hano—and one below to the east of the mesa, Polacca. Twelve miles to the west looms Second Mesa—which is split at its end—with its three villages: Mishongnovi, Shipaulovi, and Shongopovi. About ten miles beyond is the Third Mesa promontory, with Old Oraibi at its tip and New Oraibi, Hotevilla, and Bacobi as its offshoots.

The homeland of the Hopi is an exceedingly inhospitable desert environment—vast tracts of semiarid land, studded with buttes, mesas, canyons, and stretches of sand dunes, visited by infrequent but devastating downpours and strong windstorms. All food, fuel, and most of the water has to be laboriously borne more than half a mile up to the mesa Shipaulovi, and Shongopovi. About ten miles beyond is the Third Mesa promontory, with Old Oraibi at its tip and New Oraibi, Hotevilla, and Bacobi as its offshoots.

The homeland of the Hopi is an exceedingly inhospitable desert environment—vast tracts of semiarid land, studded with buttes, mesas, canyons, and stretches of sand dunes, visited by infrequent but devastating downpours and strong windstorms. All food, fuel, and most of the water has to be laboriously borne more than half a mile up to the mesa tops.

Woven into the very warp and woof of Hopi life is a body of ceremonials and traditions that relate to the people's wanderings after leaving the Underworld—their legendary source of origins. It was during these wanderings that the complex system of Hopi clans and clan societies came into being. Involved in every Hopi religious ceremonial is a multitude of references and symbols pertaining to these clan migrations.[2] The Hopi cosmogony embraces a Creation Myth and successive Emergences from three previous worlds to the present Fourth World.

The Hopi are agricultural, their chief food being corn. As their livelihoods are closely tied to nature, they carefully consider the proper times for planting, harvesting, hunting, and for ceremonies, weddings and many other activities. "In order to know these dates," wrote Sun Chief, a Hopi, "it was necessary to keep close watch on the sun's movements."[3]

Until the beginning of the century, visitors to Hopi territory were rare, but in the 1920s, when the tribe numbered just over two thousand, automobile campers were not an uncommon sight and travelers by rail flocked by the thousands to one of the most dramatic of rituals, the Snake Dance.

Today, the Hopi population exceeds eight thousand. Their history of stubborn resistance to outside influences and their geographic isolation have helped them to preserve many of their traditions—more so than almost any Indian group in North America.

EACH TIME A WAY OF LIFE DISAPPEARS, THE REPERTOIRE OF HUMAN EXPERIENCE IS DIMINISHED.

ALEXANDER ALLAND, JR.
(ANTHROPOLOGIST)[4]

THE HOPI UNLIMITED!

The Santa Fe's promotion of the Southwest proffered the thrill of new places and exotic but native cultures veiled with a quaint charm and picturesqueness. The potential tourist was invited to camp out inside the culture, to discover America through "the Original Americans," and to feel that he was unearthing a vital part of his heritage.

MISHONGNOVI, HOPI PUEBLO

The Pueblo Indians of the Southwest are the most communally minded builders of citylike dwellings America has yet known. The pueblos themselves are a reflection of and a response to the mountains and valleys where they are built. Dances held in their plazas express this relationship between the earth and the life that grows out of it. A remarkable system of community cooperation exists in Pueblo industry, farming, and ceremonial, or religious, life. For example, so much does the success of a ceremony depend upon the disposition of mutual helpfulness that the public announcement of a ceremony typically concludes with "We must all be kind to one another and not make one another unhappy." Furthermore, ". . . any worry, sorrow or anger disqualifies a Hopi, as a rule, to participate in a ceremony," commented the missionary H. R. Voth.[5] Little evidence of the white man's influence can be seen in this photograph. The village appears to be deserted, but quite possibly the picture was taken in the heat of the day or at harvest time, when the people were in the fields.

SHIPAULOVI, HOPI PUEBLO (SECOND MESA)

Architectural features of Pueblo homes had changed little in the two hundred years prior to 1878, when ethnologist John C. Bourke first visited the Hopi villages. He wrote the following description in his diary: "We observed on our way that the chimneys of the houses were made of earthenware pots, placed one upon another and coated with mud, that upon the roofs in nearly all cases were bake-ovens, and that to enter any house it was necessary first to ascend a ladder to the roof of the first story and then descend to the living rooms . . . the walls were not, as with us, flush with the front walls of the edifice. They receded in such a manner as to leave a platform in front; this was the roof of the first story and was formed of round pine logs, covered with small branches and afterwards plastered smoothly with mud."[6]

HOPI VILLAGE LIFE

Pueblo architecture conveys an appearance of ruggedness and antiquity. Perhaps the most noteworthy characteristic of pueblo masonry in both ancient and modern examples, writes anthropologist Victor Mindeleff, is "the use of small chinking stones for bringing the masonry to an even face after the larger stones forming the body of the wall have been laid in place."[7] The stone masonry seen here retains some of the peculiarities that characterize ancient stonework. For example, the interstices between the large stones were plugged with small fragments, which were then driven in with stone hammers, producing a fairly even face of masonry. Afterward, mud plaster was applied, a handful at a time.[8] Such construction was not the most practical in the Pueblo climate. Violent storms played havoc with the earth-covered houses, necessitating constant vigilance and frequent repairs.

HOPI MENDING MOCCASINS, PUEBLO OF ORAIBI

Amongst the Hopi pueblos, there was no such thing as a village shoemaker. Every man made his own or went barefoot. In this picture, the moccasin maker is busy applying his awl and sinew as he completes the mending of the commonplace but indispensable Hopi foot covering. The woman of the household does her best to shun the camera politely. Hopi sewing skills were exceptional; they employed a form of "invisible mending" in which the stitches were well hidden and never showed. The tanned leather was stained a warm brown, red, or black; the dyes came from the resin and bark of trees and local clays.

THE MOCCASIN MAKER, ORAIBI. ANOTHER VIEW

The moccasin maker threads his awl while his companion softens the leather. Even today, a special pair of new moccasins is a necessary part of a Hopi bride's trousseau. For the biennial sacred ceremony of the Snake Dance, the Snake priests require a reserve of moccasins. Tourists can have them made on the spot. Fringe and strings may be added to the leather, as well as silver buttons made from dimes or quarters.

HOPI BOYS

Young boys were sent out to herd sheep whenever the livestock were corralled near the mesa. (Here, one child is holding a herding stick.) Boys were taught that "work means life" and that "it was a disgrace to be idle." Sun Chief, a Hopi, speaks about his childhood at Oraibi, in a cherished land of "mesa air, spiced with spruce and pine": "We followed our fathers to the fields and helped plant and weed. The old men took us for walks and taught us the use of plants and how to collect them . . . . We watched the fields to drive out the birds and rodents, helped pick peaches to dry in the sun, and gathered melons to lug up the mesa. We rode burros to harvest corn, gather fuel or herd sheep."[9]

HOPI GIRLS WITH BABIES

At the age of eight or ten, girls were entrusted with the care of their younger brothers and sisters, and it was not an uncommon sight to see them going about their chores with babies slung over their shoulders in a sheet or blanket. As young children, little girls played with small grinding stones in preparation for adult life. They were taught very early to grind corn and were often asked to display their accomplishments before visitors. A constant reminder was a Hopi proverb: "Corn is the Hopi heart." Hopi girls learned to be proud of their grinding skills, the result of which would be a bountiful supply of cornmeal, the staff of life for the family.

THE MEN WERE WARNED NOT TO ATTEMPT TO TAKE ANY PICTURES, EVEN THOUGH THE BRIGHT MOON WOULD PERMIT IT. THERE WERE TWO BUSLOADS ON THE TOUR, AND AS THEY DREW UP TO THE PUEBLO, FULLY HALF THE MEN GRABBED THEIR CAMERAS, JUMPED OFF THE BUS, AND STARTED SNAPPING AWAY AT THE DANCING INDIANS. WITHOUT A SOUND, INDIANS POURED OUT OF EVERY DOORWAY, ALL CARRYING CLUBS. THE TWO DRIVERS LIT OUT AT A DEAD RUN TO ROUND UP THE SCATTERING MEN, BUT BEFORE THEY COULD GET THEM BACK ON THE BUSES, THERE WAS A GENERAL SMASHING OF CAMERAS THAT STARTED BY KNOCKING THEM TO THE GROUND WITH CLUBS AND THEN JUMPING UP AND DOWN ON THEM.

D. H. THOMAS
(OCCASION OF THE HAPPINESS DANCE,
SANTO DOMINGO PUEBLO, 1926)[10]

FLEEING FROM THE CAMERA, HOPI

Many Indians refused to be photographed. It was their view that a portrait would bring bad luck, shorten their lives, and lead to their death. It was also believed that in the relinquishment of one's image, one's power was dissipated. And if that happened, one was left with nothing and was thought to be defenseless.

In recent years, a camera permit has been required in all Hopi villages, and visitors have been banned from most religious ceremonies. Social or secular dances, however, may be observed and remain as popular as ever.

HOPI WOMAN WITH WATER JAR AND CARRYING BURDEN

The Indians first called photographers "shadow catchers" because of the photograph's remarkable power to capture irrevocably their restless shadows. The white man's ability to use the sun to transfix their images was regarded by the Indians with awe and suspicion. Indians also believed it dangerous to tamper with the mysterious power—one manifestation of which was the sun. Mato-Kuwapi, or Chased-by-Bears, observed: " . . . when we see the changes of day and night, the sun, moon, and stars in the sky, and the changing seasons upon the earth, with their ripening fruits, anyone must realize that it is the work of the sun, without which we could not live . . . ."[11] The Hopi woman shown in this photograph clearly did not wish to be photographed.

HOPI MOTHER AND CHILD, MISHONGNOVI

From the moment they are born, children are of central importance in Hopi life. They are very much desired by the Hopi. Girls, in particular, hold a special place within Hopi society, as they are an assurance of the perpetuation of the clan. Children belong to their mother's clan, and their closest connections, from birth to death, remain with it. During the first twenty days of a child's existence, a perfect ear of white corn is placed on either side of the infant when he is on the cradle board. One represents the mother, the other, the baby. They are called "mother corn ears" and are regarded as sacred.[12]

WOMAN MAKING POTTERY, MOKI PUEBLO, ARIZONA

This Hopi woman is making pottery, using the "coiling technique." Even "ropes" of clay are rolled out from her palms and coiled into the desired shape. Work on the vessel begins in a concave dish held in her lap called a tabipi, *which turns easily on its curved bottom. The tabipi serves the function of a potter's wheel. Hopi superstition holds that when the time arrives for the firing of the pottery, if anyone should speak above a whisper, the spirit inhabiting the vessel will cause it to break.*[13]

HOPI BLANKET WEAVER, ORAIBI

Among the Hopi, unlike the Navajo, weaving is the exclusive occupation of men. They used to weave all the community's clothing. Hopi men are also farmers and herders, and they tend to the religious matters of the community. It is in the kiva that they card and spin wool and weave blankets, kilts, belts, and heavy black mantas (women's dresses). "While they are spinning," wrote a Hopi, Crow-wing, in his journal in 1920, "one man will tell the teöwichi [folktales or myths]. All have to listen to him. When he finishes, another man will tell, and so on until afternoon when the women will bring food. . . . They will start again and then the old man will tell the men about the way the people came to the mesa and how they must mind Hopi customs."[14]

HOPI WOMEN AT WORK COILING BASKETS AT HOPI HOUSE, GRAND CANYON

Hopi House was built on the rim of the Grand Canyon, right across from the luxurious El Tovar Hotel. It opened on January 1, 1905, and was said to "symbolize the partnership between commercialism and romanticism that typified so much of Fred Harvey architecture."[15] Hopi House was a re-creation of a section of the Hopi village of Oraibi. There Navajo, Hopi, and Zuni artisans wove baskets and blankets, made jewelry and pottery, carved trinkets, and spun wool. The coiled plaques and baskets shown in the photograph were woven by the Hopi women of Second Mesa. Their flair for color is very much in evidence here, reflected in the abstract figures of animals, kachinas, and crops, which are woven into the overall basket design. At Hopi House, all items were for sale and there, "on the patio at five," Indian groups sang and danced for the tourists.

THE RED PEPPER LADY, HOPI

Indians reveal much about their land, history, and philosophy in their basketry. Baskets were an essential part of every household; they were used to winnow grain, parch corn, haul wood, and collect wild foods. Woven baskets were awarded as prizes, given as gifts, and used as money.

The Hopi woman is holding in her lap a wicker basket typical of Third Mesa work. Behind her are the colorful ristratas of drying chili peppers.

This photograph became a popular image on thousands of postcards printed by W.H. Jackson's Detroit Publishing Company. A large portion of the more than two million postcards produced annually by the company was purchased by the Santa Fe Railway for their promotion of the American Southwest.

HOPI INDIAN GIRLS GRINDING

Mealing troughs for grinding corn were indispensable items in every Hopi household. They were described by one observer as "a series of three flat slabs of sandstone about fifteen inches square, cemented at a convenient angle for the worker."[16] From the age of eight or so, young girls knelt at the mealing troughs crushing the grains with their manos, or oblong hand stones, until they reduced the coarse fragments of corn to fine flour. The troughs were of graded coarseness, as were the manos. A grinder rubbed up and down upon the slabs, much like a woman at her washboard. While at work, gossip was exchanged, perspiring faces were powdered with meal, and grinding songs were sung which spoke of "excellent growing corn" and "rain com[ing]."[17]

IT'S THE POWER OF BELIEF WHICH MAKES ALL THE DIFFERENCE BE-
TWEEN ORIGINAL NATIVE ART AND CONTEMPORARY NATIVE CRAFTS.
FROELICH RAINEY (ARCHAEOLOGIST)[18]

A HOSTILE! A PUEBLO POTTER MIXING CLAY

Pottery making in the Southwest has been an important activity for at least two thousand years. It is a vital industry in a number of pueblos, each of which produces a highly differentiated ware. The potter's wheel is unknown, and all pottery is still made by the coiling technique. Traditionally, pottery was made essentially for household purposes. It assumed a new function at the beginning of this century, when the tourists' acquisitiveness for pottery became so great that the demand nearly exceeded the supply. Pueblo potters, writes anthropologist Ruth Bunzel, are guided entirely by their tactile sense and an unconscious feeling for proportion. "From no woman in any pueblo did I get any rule of proportions," she reported in 1924. ". . . The most general principles I could elicit were: 'It must be even all around, not larger on one side than another. . . .'" Theirs was a sentient approach rather than a quantitative one and "we must therefore believe the potter," continued Bunzel, "when she says, 'I carry all the designs in my head and never get them mixed up.'"[19]

(One would assume that irony was intended in the picture's title.)

HOPI HAIRDRESSING

This charming trio of pictures reveals that it was a laborious task, indeed, to arrange one's hair in the ancient coiffure required for a Hopi maiden. The locks are formed into two large, upstanding whorls on each side of the head and shaped into the hairstyle that is characteristic of the unmarried status of a young woman. The whorl is symbolic of the squash blossom, which signifies both the Hopi symbol of purity and "the potential power of fructification." The wearing of this coiffure comes from great antiquity. According to anthropologist Jesse Walter Fewkes, early Spanish explorers observed the custom in ancient pictographs.

The first step in the creation of the maiden's hairstyle is to arrange the hair on a U-shaped stick called, in Hopi, a gñela. The hair is then given body with an oil pressed from squash seeds that causes it to stiffen, "making a frame which looks like an old-fashioned headdress."[20] After a period of time, the gñelas are removed, leaving two large puffs just above the ears and held in place with tightly wound string. The surprisingly large, glossy whorls are commonly referred to as "wheels."

Fewkes stated that ". . . in some of the figurines used in connection with modern Hopi altars these whorls are represented by small wheels made of sticks radiating from a common juncture and connected by woolen yarn." Fewkes also provided a fascinating parallel when he noted that "the country women in Salamanca, Spain, do their hair up in two flat coils, one on each side of the forehead, a custom [the Spaniards] may have had in mind when [they] compared the Pueblo coiffure to an 'old-fashioned headdress.'"[21]

HOPI MAIDEN LOOKING OUT OF WINDOW

INDIAN GIRL ON LADDER, HOPI

MARRIED AND UNMARRIED HOPI WOMEN

Hairstyle defined roles and conferred significance in Hopi life. The difference between the hairstyles of married and unmarried women provides a dramatic example. Upon betrothal, a maiden relinquished her elaborate whorls and wore her hair in the fashion common to matrons: down, parted in the middle, and worn in two rolls wound with dark cotton string.

HOPI WEDDING DRESS

This Hopi bride is dressed in traditional wedding garments: a robe of white cotton, woven by the men of the bridegroom's family (his clan uncles), and white deerskin moccasins and leggings. She also holds a reed "suitcase" that contains a second, smaller, robe (also white) and a finely woven belt. The bride will be buried in this robe, which is carefully preserved until her death. Both the robe and the belt serve as "wings to speed her to dear ones in the House of the Dead . . . the beautiful belt . . . serv[ing] as tail to a bird, guiding the bride in her spiritual flight."[22]

HOPI HARVEST DANCE

> "With their corn growing
> power they come. . . ." [23]

In the life of a Hopi, almost as much effort is expended in worship as in work. In an environment where survival is difficult, all prosperity depends upon propitiating the deities. The Harvest Dance is a large and popular communal pageant in celebration of the ripening season. Its objective is a successful harvest and ripe corn. It is also a ceremony of thanksgiving for the fruits bestowed by Mother Earth. This colorful dance was a favorite subject of the photographers and was immortalized on thousands of postcards issued by the Detroit Publishing Company.

THE KACHINAS

"In the summer katcinas with great heads and fine clothes came into the plaza and danced. . . . The katcinas usually gave us gifts. At about sundown . . . an old man, called the Father of the Katcinas . . . asked them to go home and send us rain. They marched away toward the San Francisco mountains in the west. Everybody knew they were spirit gods."[24]

The *kachina* dances are spectacular displays of color and costume and are very popular in all the Pueblo villages. The kachina dancers are believed to be the embodiments of supernatural beings and mythic characters, including animals, birds, and ancestors. The dances are both social and religious in nature and are performed masked and unmasked. They objectify the external world of the Pueblo Indian and instruct the young. Emory Sekaquaptewa, a contemporary Hopi participant in the ceremony, writes about the spiritual center of this experience. "The use of the mask in the kachina ceremony has more than just an esthetic purpose. I feel that what happens to a man when he is a performer is that if he understands the essence of the kachina, when he dons the mask he loses his identity and actually becomes what he is representing. . . . The spiritual fulfillment of a man depends on how he is able to project himself into the spiritual world as he performs. He really doesn't perform for the third parties who form the audience. Rather the audience becomes his personal self. He tries to express to himself his own conceptions about the spiritual ideals that he sees in the kachina. He is able to do so behind the mask because he has lost his personal identity. . . . But the essence of the kachina ceremony for me as a participant has to do with the ability to project oneself into the make-believe world, the world of ideas and images which sustain that particular representation."[25]

A kachina dance is performed with the expectation that it will bring rain and that it will enhance the general well-being of the people. In his autobiography Sun Chief, a Hopi, writes: "A dance may [also] be sponsored by an individual who wishes to receive a special blessing such as recovery from a disease, or to insure the prosperity of the entire village."[26]

Young children first become acquainted with kachina symbols in the form of dolls. More than two hundred and fifty different kinds exist. The dolls shown on the following pages were probably produced for tourists. They were items in great demand and continue to be popular today.

HOPI KACHINA DOLLS

At left is a Third Mesa Big Head Kachina. He wears a datura flower (jimsonweed) on one side and vertical feathers on the other, green moccasins, and black, yellow, and red body paint. He brings gentle rain without thunder. In the center: This wooden figure resembles the Hemis, or "Home Dance," kachina, with an elaborate tablita (headdress) painted with phallic and cloud symbols. The Hemis, a homecoming festival for Hopi everywhere, is an especially festive occasion for children, for at this time the kachinas bring great quantities of peaches, melons, corn, beans, and other gifts—including new kachina dolls. It is also the event at which eligible brides make their appearance and at which men "break spruce boughs from the costumes of the Katcinas and plant them in their fields with prayers for their crops . . . ."[27] At right is a Mustard Green Kachina. Red ears and black warrior marks on the cheeks are the outstanding features.[28]

HOPI KACHINA DOLLS

At the left is the Heheya Kachina. Its important distinguishing marks are a green case, or helmet mask, cloud symbols on the cheeks, and vertical zigzag lines on the face, which represent lightning. At the center: This carved figure gives every indication of being a clown; the absence of a case mask, the lack of clothing, horizontal body stripes, and a white face mask are the characteristic features. This carving has a very aggressive posture. The clown serves to entertain and ridicule the spectators between the dances and while the kachinas are resting, and he often plays the role of ribald prankster, much to everyone's delight. Clowns also serve as an important social-control factor. Clowns are the teachers. Through their buffoonery, they enforce communal discipline. They also "loosen everything up, all of creation, of which we are a part, so that it can lose its inhibitions and rain."[29]
At the right is a mixture of Shalako and Butterfly Kachinas. In producing kachinas for the tourist market, it was not an uncommon practice to blend the features of various kachinas. In this example, the white face mask, cloud symbols and multicolored chin of the Shalako were combined with the rectangular eyes and red body paint of the Butterfly Kachina.

IF WE COULD PICK THE THREADS OF RELIGION FROM THE WARP AND WOOF OF HOPI LIFE THERE APPARENTLY WOULD NOT BE MUCH LEFT.

WALTER HOUGH (ETHNOLOGIST, 1915)[30]

CEREMONIES ARE THE BOND THAT HOLDS THE MULTITUDES TOGETHER, AND IF THE BOND BE REMOVED, THOSE MULTITUDES FALL INTO CONFUSION.

BOOK OF RITES (THE LI CHI)[31]

THE HOPI SNAKE DANCE CEREMONY

The Snake Dance stretched its unrelenting mystery across the vaulted skies. It was a dramatized prayer to the heavens to weep generously upon the dry, cracked earth of the desert floor. The biennial ritual gave order to the Hopi world. It was a way of controlling, of giving shape and significance to, an otherwise incomprehensible universe. It explained the phenomena of nature and aided the Hopi in knowing the unknown. It tapped superhuman power.

The Snake Dance first began to catch the attention of tourists in the 1890s. A. C. Vromans, the noted Southwest photographer, recorded the ceremony between 1895 and 1902 in the Hopi villages of Walpi, Oraibi, and Mishongnovi. Vromans kept extensive notes of his impressions. He first observed the ceremony at Walpi and wrote in his diary: "We found some forty white people camped, all to see the dance. Was not a little surprised to learn these were artists of note. Authors, sculptors, newspaper correspondents from a half dozen papers and some dozen or more ladies."[32] Some years later, Theodore Roosevelt also witnessed the dance at Walpi. He, too, commented on the visitors. Of his experience in 1913, he tells us that he "did not happen to run across any Mormons at the Snake Dance; but it seemed every other class of Americans was represented, tourists, traders, cattlemen, farmers, Government officials, politicians, cowboys, scientists, philanthropists, all kinds of men and women."[33] Two years later, anthropologist Walter Hough wrote that it was "well worth braving the journey to see . . . one of the most impressive spectacles that can be witnessed on this continent."[34] For many spectators, however, the Snake Dance evoked ambivalent reactions. A popular lecturer described his fascination with the "weird chant[ing]" and "squirming reptiles" in his account of the "repulsive Snake Dance."[35] By the 1920s, the Snake Dance had been heavily publicized as a major attraction of Southwest Indian life. The Santa Fe Railway promoted it as a "bizarre spectacle" and the "weirdest and most impressive aboriginal ritual of the American continent."[36] In 1927 special motor cruises to and from the event were offered to the "discriminating traveler" (at indiscriminate prices). The spectacle of the aboriginal's cosmic universe was turned into a consumer commodity. With it came the promise of excitement, even dread.

There was nothing familiar about the Snake ceremony. The tourist crossed a threshold of total strangeness. For this reason, the Snake Dance was an unfailing attraction. Visitors came in the thousands with strangely jumbled anticipations. Primal in its evocation, the ceremony summoned up "the recollection of things to come" and invisible currents of power. The experience was an arrest in time, where "once you entered . . . the scale of all things changed. . . . The smallness, the limitations ceased to exist. . . . Primitive world, where shapes that are small suddenly loom up large, gigantic on the shadow . . . "[37]

More recently, several villages have closed the Snake Dance to all whites and any drunken Indians, the inevitable response to the sideshow atmosphere created by audiences intent only upon the sensational.

THERE STILL REMAIN THE TERRIFYING UNDER-DEEPS, OF WHICH WE HAVE UTTERLY NO EXPERIENCE.

D. H. LAWRENCE[38]

SUPELA, HOPI SNAKE PRIEST, PUEBLO OF WALPI

Supela, the Snake priest, appears only in partial costume, and his body paint has not yet been applied. He is wearing the brown leather snake kilt with the symbol of the snake on it; around his waist is tied a wide girth, or belt, consisting of a piece of buckskin cut into long fringes; the leg bands, worn below the knee, are made of deer-leg skin, and the arm bands are made of either green cedar bark or cedar wood. Of this unique and "mirthful" individual, ethnologist Walter Hough wrote: " . . . it seems that no observance in Walpi can get along without [Supela's] aid, and even the farther towns often call upon him to assist them in delicate points involved in the conduct of their religious celebrations. . . . [Supela] resembles a promoter or a ward politician and covers more ground in a day than [most] could in a week."[39]

THE SNAKE KIVA—HOPI

A sign has been erected on the kiva ladder, warning all visitors to stay away because preparations for the ceremony are underway. Above the sign, the bow standard decked with sacred prayer feathers is displayed—a protection from all evil influences that might enter the kiva and a signal for quiet and respect.

At the lower right are digging sticks and hoes that have been brought from the fields to be used in hunting the snakes for the ceremony. The priests leave the kiva on four successive days to gather snakes. Equipped with snake whips made of eagle feathers and bags of corn for offerings at shrines along the route, they carry buffalo-skin bags in which to put the snakes. All varieties of snakes are gathered, including bull snakes, ribbon snakes, and rattlers. Upon finding the first four snakes, prayer-feather offerings are made. The snakes are addressed: "My son, also my father . . . May rain speedily come, do not be angry, do not bite. I am thankful to find you."[40] After the prayer offerings are made, the sacred cornmeal is sprinkled upon the snakes.

ENTRANCE TO THE KIVA

Two Snake priests enter the kiva carrying bundles of feathers with which to make the pahos, *or feathered prayer sticks. During the eight days prior to the public performance of the Snake Dance, a variety of activities takes place in the kiva, including praying, ceremonial smoking, the practice of religious songs, and the repairing of moccasins, Snake Dance kilts, and other ritual paraphernalia. The men erect an altar and make a sand painting. During this time, the many snake whips required for the ceremony are made from the eagle feathers.*

TWO HOPI RACERS

In preparation for the Snake Dance, a foot race is held before dawn on the eighth morning. The race is a fantastic display of speed and endurance. The winner receives a symbolic jar of water to pour on his fields, as well as pahos, which he places near his corn plants to assure a good crop. The whole village rises and assembles for this event. Theodore Roosevelt, a spectator in 1913, later wrote: "Before there was a hint of dawn, we heard the voice of the crier summoning the runners to get ready, . . . and we rose and made our way to the mesa top . . . and watched the women and children in their ceremonial finery looking . . . for the return of the racers . . . Many of [the women] were in their white bridal dresses. . . . The returning racers ran at speed up the precipitous paths to the mesa, although it was the close of a six-mile run. . . . I should like to have entered that easy-breathing winner in a Marathon contest!"[41]

SNAKE PRIESTS LEAVING KIVA WITH PRAYER STICKS AND BAGS OF CORN

Before dawn on the ninth day, the Snake priests make their way out of the kiva to the plaza and then descend the steep mesa trails to the starting place of the second race of the Snake Society. Pahos are deposited at shrines along the route of the race, as well as at the starting point. In like manner, sacred cornmeal is scattered at intervals along the way. Some of the Snake priests twirl "bullroarers," noisemaking devices that create the impression of thunder, while others fling wooden "lightning frames" back and forth to simulate lightning. In both instances, the priests are impersonating Sotukinangwu'u, chief sky god of the Hopi. [42]

THE BEGINNING IS PURIFICATION. . . . THAT'S A BIG STEP AND IT'S SERIOUS BUSINESS. THERE'S A RIGHT WAY TO DO EVERYTHING, AND THERE'S A RIGHT WAY TO PURIFICATION. IT'S COMPLETELY NATURAL, I'LL TELL YOU THAT MUCH. THERE'S NOTHING ARTIFICIAL. AND PURIFICATION MEANS PURIFICATION OF BODY AND MIND. YOU DON'T PURIFY THE BODY WITHOUT CLEANSING THE MIND: THAT'S THE WAY IT WORKS.

. . . SO WE BEGIN BY WATCHING OUR WORDS AND SPEAKING WITH GOOD PURPOSE ONLY.

ROLLING THUNDER (MEDICINE MAN)[43]

SNAKE PRIESTS, ORAIBI

During the late afternoon of the eighth day, all the priests leave the kiva for a ceremonial bathing ritual. They wash their heads in foaming yucca-root suds to cleanse and purify their bodies and spirits in preparation for the ceremony of the washing of the reptiles the next day. The entire Snake Dance ceremony, performed by both the Antelope and Snake clans, is an expression of the Hopi identification with various animal species.[44]

WE KNEW SNAKES WERE SPIRIT GODS WHO BRING RAIN AND NEVER HARM ANYONE WITH A GOOD HEART. WE WERE TOLD NEVER TO ACT SILLY AND SCREAM OR YELL LIKE WHITES WHEN A SNAKE GOES TOWARD THEM. WHEN SNAKES WERE PLEASED WITH THEIR TREATMENT THEY WERE QUIET AND WOULD BRING RAIN AS A REWARD.

SUN CHIEF (HOPI)[45]

THE SNAKES, OF COURSE, TRY TO ESCAPE BUT ARE PUSHED BACK WITH WHIPS....BUT IN SPITE OF ALL THESE MEASURES THE SNAKES MAKE DESPERATE EFFORTS TO ESCAPE, NOT ONLY THE RACERS THAT GLIDE SWIFTLY UP AND DOWN, BUT ALSO THE BULL AND RATTLE SNAKES. THEY CRAWL OVER AND BETWEEN THE NUDE LEGS OF THE MEN, UP THEIR ARMS, ETC., SO THAT IT OFTEN BECOMES NECESSARY TO TAKE THEM WITH THE HAND AND LAY THEM BACK. AS THE NUMBER OF REPTILES INCREASE, IT BECOMES MORE DIFFICULT TO CONTROL THEM AND KEEP THEM ON THE SMALL PLACE ASSIGNED TO THEM, AND FOR A TIME THE MEN ARE KEPT VERY BUSY. THE SNAKES, FINDING ALL THEIR EFFORTS TO ESCAPE FRUSTRATED, FINALLY HUDDLE TOGETHER IN THE TWO CORNERS. IT IS SIMPLY APPALLING WITH WHAT APPARENT UNCONCERN THOSE MEN HANDLE THE REPTILES.

H. R. VOTH (MISSIONARY AND ETHNOLOGIST)[46]

THE WASHING OF THE SNAKES IN SNAKE KIVA

On the morning of the ninth day, a ceremonial washing of the snakes takes place. This event is considered to be "one of the most weird and unique rites throughout the ceremony." During the solemn occasion, the snakes are dipped, one at a time, into a large container of yucca-root lather. Afterward, they are placed in the sand on the kiva floor to dry. As Theodore Roosevelt recorded at Walpi in 1913, "eighty or a hundred snakes . . . were hurled to the floor from a distance of a dozen feet. . . . The unexpected violence . . . ought to have upset the nerves of every snake there. However, it did not . . . the snakes . . . writhed themselves free of one another . . . and began to slide rapidly in every direction. But only one showed symptoms of anger, and these were not marked."[47] Voth voiced the same puzzlement: "How is it possible that one of these snakes, that is taken hold of again and again, and with such recklessness, does not strike, when from forty to fifty are confined on such a small space?"[48]

ANTELOPE PRIESTS ENTERING AND CIRCLING THE PLAZA

In the late afternoon of the ninth day, the Antelope priests enter the plaza and then circle it four times, shaking their rattles and moving to the loud moaning sound of the bullroarer. This picture shows the variety of spectators who attended the dance, including numerous photographers. Overcrowding was a serious problem because of the extra weight of the visitors that the roofs and the walls of the pueblo were forced to support. The large influx of white onlookers also became a matter of concern, for they seriously threatened the devout meaning of the ritual. " . . . When gazed upon by so many strangers," wrote ethnologist Jesse Walter Fewkes in 1901, "some of the Snake men appeared to be more nervous and did not handle the reptiles in the fearless manner which marked earlier performances."[49]

SNAKE PRIESTS CIRCLING THE PLAZA

With the arrival of the Snake priests, the atmosphere ignites, nearly splitting the air. They enter and move about the plaza in a vigorous "jump trot," wearing fox skins and leather kilts embroidered with a serpent design and carrying, in their right hands, snake whips made from eagle feathers. The "long line of Snake men dance like [the] writhing of [a] serpent," wrote Alexander M. Stephen in his Hopi Journal, *the "line swaying out and in, men singing in low measure . . . a slow solemn dirgelike moan." All the while, the Antelope priests keep time with their rattles. In this picture, the Snake dancers are about to take their positions opposite the Antelopes in front of the kisi, a leafy cottonwood brush house where the snakes are concealed.*

A STRICT LAW BIDS US DANCE.
KWAKIUTL OBSERVATION[50]

WE DO NOT BELIEVE OUR RELIGION, WE DANCE IT!
A NATIVE AMERICAN[51]

THERE ARE PLACES NO HISTORY CAN REACH.
NORMAN MAILER[52]

THE HOPI SNAKE DANCE FILM

The following film sequence of the Hopi Snake Dance was shot at the pueblo of Walpi, circa 1912, by a Santa Fe Railway advertising executive and photographer, William E. Kopplin. It is rare footage—a glimpse of life as it really was. There are but a handful of moving pictures that show the ceremony as it was performed near the turn of the century. The Santa Fe used the Snake Dance film as a promotional and educational tool. Representatives were sent across the country to show it to church groups and colleges, and to tourists in the Lecture Lounges of the Santa Fe/Harvey hotels. The showings offered an exotic flight into another culture and stimulated travel on the Santa Fe line.

Many frustrations and hardships were suffered in filming Indians in the Southwest. The environment presented difficult challenges for the cameraman: On the desert plateaus, sudden windstorms and flash floods wreaked violence upon equipment and supplies, often wiping out long hours of arduous work. The killing heat brought excruciating discomfort. The potential for havoc was increased by intense competition for the best camera positions. There are stories of ugly squabbles for prime locations that resulted in camera stands being kicked over and equipment ruined. The cameramen also faced severe technical challenges. The limited sensitivity of the films used in early motion-picture cameras required stronger light than was available in the late afternoon, when the Snake Dance took place. In addition to the dexterity needed to maintain the focus of moving subjects under such adverse light conditions, the cameramen also had to turn the camera crank at constant but varying speeds—at times "undercranking" to speed up action on the screen and then "overcranking" to slow it down. All these adjustments had to be made on the run in order to keep up with the positions of the dancers. Even the most persistent and devoted professionals ran into snags. "The threading was complicated and the thing frequently jammed," reported an early cameraman.[53] Moreover, the Indian's superstitions about photography, and their growing suspicions of the motives of the photographers who streamed through their world and invaded their privacy, contributed to an increasing reluctance to allow themselves to become subjects of the white man's curiosity.

The film frames in the following pages set forth a substantial part of the sacred rites of the Hopi Snake Dance.

FRAME 1:   The Antelope priests enter the plaza first.

FRAME 2:   They circle the plaza four times, sprinkling sacred meal.

FRAME 3:   *The Snake priests follow.*

FRAME 4:   *The Snake priests repeat the four circuits with fierce energy.*

FRAME 5:   *The priests line up at the kisi, where the snakes are kept.*

FRAME 6:   *When the singing stops, the Snake priests move toward the kisi.*

FRAME 7: *Within seconds, some priests (the "carriers") emerge with the snakes.*

FRAME 8: *The dance commences; snakes dangle from each carrier's mouth.*

FRAME 9:   *The gatherers are kept busy catching the snakes.*

FRAME 10:   *The spectators are awed as the number of reptiles multiplies.*

FRAME 11: *Photographers (center background) strive to get their pictures.*

FRAME 12: *Dancers reach for remaining snakes in the kisi.*

FRAME 13:   *The gatherers control escaping reptiles amid an increasingly excited crowd.*

FRAME 14:   *The snakes are flung together in a pile at Snake Rock.*

FRAME 15: *The dancers ingest a bitter emetic, a purifier that induces vomiting.*

Frame 1

The Antelope dancers enter the plaza shaking their rattles. White zigzag lines on their backs, chests, and legs represent streaks of lightning. Their kilts are of richly embroidered white cotton, each with a multicolored sash. A white line painted from ear to ear extends over the upper lip. The large boulder at the right side of the picture is Snake Rock, also called The Great Altar Rock, in the vicinity of which the Snake ceremony always takes place.

Frame 2

The head priest of the Antelope Society carries a basket of sacred cornmeal, which he sprinkles about as he circles the plaza. Each dancer holds a rattle in his right hand and carries a gourd of the sacred cornmeal, which is also dispersed at various shrines throughout the plaza. The leafy kisi at the left, a small enclosed "booth" fashioned from cottonwood boughs and long reeds, holds the snakes. In front of the kisi, a rough plank covers a hole in the ground, called the sipapu, representing the entrance to the Underworld, wherein dwell the spirits the dancers must attract. With each circuit, the ancers vigorously stamp on the sipapu.

Frames 3 and 4

As the Snake priests enter, the mood in the plaza changes. A moment of tremendous drama unfolds as they trot in, bodies stained to near-black, daubed with splotches and spots of white clay, chins whitened, and carrying snake whips made of eagle feathers in their right hands. The Snake men repeat the four circuits with a fierce energy and then take their positions opposite the Antelope dancers.

Frame 5

As evidenced by this picture, it had become fashionable at the turn of the century to attend the "weird," "bizarre," and even "repulsive" Snake Dance. Tourists were everywhere and were already becoming a serious threat to the sacred nature of the rituals. Add to this the general confusion created by the competing photographers, and it is not difficult to imagine the ceremony coming to resemble a theatrical show with a circus atmosphere, turning a most hallowed rite into a histrionic performance.

Frames 6 and 7

When the singing stops, the Snake priests—"carriers" and "huggers"—move in pairs toward the kisi and stoop down; the carriers emerge within seconds, with snakes hanging from their mouths. Some of them handle the reptiles first, as can be seen in the left middle ground of Frame 7, before taking them into their mouths. Together, carrier and hugger commence the dance around the plaza, and the chanting resumes. Meanwhile, the gatherers waste no time in corralling and picking up any straying snakes. For the Hopi people, there is a natural connection between the snakes and rain, where "the symbol of lightning is a zig-zag line much like the movement of a snake. Out of this similarity grew the concept of snakes as messengers of the deities."[54]

Frames 8 and 9

The companion priest dances with his left arm around the snake carrier's neck, and with his eagle feathers he makes a stroking motion over the snake. In 1895 Vromans observed and reported that "the Snake carrier danced with his eyes shut . . . while he carried the snake in his mouth. When he would make the circuit of the plaza twice, he would drop his snake and pick up others that other dancers had dropped, and so it would continue. . . . At times one dancer would have half a dozen snakes in his hands and mouth. They would always straighten the snake out with their snake whips . . . before attempting to pick them up. . . . When held in the hand they paid no more attention to them [than] if they were so many pieces of rope."[55]

Frame 10

The spectators watch in awe as the number of reptiles grows, and many of them dangle docilely from the lips of the dancers. In 1903 another observer of the dance, the missionary H.R. Voth, wrote that he had "seen dancers hold two, three, and on one occasion even four snakes at one time between the teeth, the reptiles intertwining into a ball . . . in front of the dancer's mouth. On one occasion [he] saw a snake that was held about mid-way of its length trying to get into the ears and nose of the dancer; several times [he] noticed a man having stuffed a small snake into his mouth entirely, the head of the reptile only protruding between his lips."[56]

Frames 11, 12, and 13

Photographers hurriedly snap away in center background as the dancers reach for the remaining snakes in the kisi; by this time the plaza has become one writhing mass of serpents. "Mr. Hunt and Mr. Mumson [Vromans' assistants] were so wrapped up in watching the dancers," wrote Vromans, "that they forgot all about their cameras, and at one point, I had seven cameras to work from my point of view . . . ."[57] The growing thunder and commotion of the dancers as the reptiles multiplied in number contributed to the increasing excitement and noise of the crowds pressing in on the plaza and hugging the rooftops, reported Vromans. In a group (in Frame 13), many gatherers, with handfuls of snakes, work at controlling the serpents.

Frame 14

When all the snakes from the kisi have been dispersed, the dancers follow the chief priest to the base of the Great Altar Rock, where the gathered snakes are thrown into a circle in one huge pile, which becomes, as one observer noted, "a horrible, hideous, wriggling mass." Within moments, the Snake men quickly seize as many snakes as they can from the pile and dash, with handfuls of the writhing reptiles, at full speed down the mesa trails. The snakes are released to the four cardinal directions as messengers to the deities.[58] The presence of a motion-picture machine can be seen in the middle background.

Frame 15

After they have removed their costumes, returned them to the kiva, and washed off their body paint, the Snake priests drink a bitter emetic, which induces profuse vomiting. This purification ritual is said to cleanse them from the snake charm, so once again they can mingle with other inhabitants of the village. Vromans wrote in 1897: "To see some thirty men drink from ollas and lean over the mesa to vomit, straining every nerve to eject the poison that may have entered the system, was no laughing matter even to onlookers. Then one by one," continued Vromans, "they retired to their homes and we began to realize that we were still in America. One becomes so interested, so anxious to see it all, that he almost forgets, and it seems like a dream."[59]

EDGE OF THE MESA, AFTER THE SNAKE DANCE

A purification ritual takes place on the edge of the mesa after the release of the snakes over the trails. Each priest drinks an emetic to purge his digestive system of salivary secretions elicited by the repeated grasping of the snakes in his mouth. The emetic also acts as a purgative of any evil effects of the snake handling. The Snake priests also chew a mixture of clay and weeds to cleanse their mouths. In the photograph above, at least four photographers are recording this final aspect of the Snake ceremony.

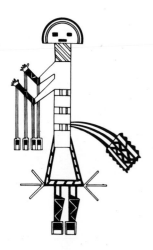

CROPS CAN BE REPLANTED. STOCK CAN REPRODUCE. SO CAN HUMAN
BEINGS. BUT THE LAND IS NOT LIKE THESE. ONCE IT IS TAKEN AWAY,
IT IS GONE FOREVER.

NAVAJO COUNCILMAN[1]

THE NAVAJO

"I was always working. That's the reason they thought I was the best Indian alive. . . ."[1a]

The Navajo and Pueblo Indians live in essentially the same physical environment, a country of rock wastes, intense aridity, and astonishing physical beauty. The Navajo are widely scattered over their area of settlement. There is not the concentration of population, the clustering of families into villages, that is characteristic of Pueblo settlement. Navajos inhabit an area of about twenty-five thousand square miles in northwestern New Mexico and northeastern Arizona. Lofty mountains such as the Lukachukai and Carrizo ranges, deep beautiful canyons including the glowing, watered sanctuary of Canyon de Chelly, a river—the San Juan—that furnishes limitless possibilities for irrigation, and vast expanses of desert extend across the Navajo's territory. It is plateau country too, where "the sky is [the] roof of the world" and "every mesa [is] duplicated by a cloud mesa, like a reflection."[2] Today the Navajo number more than one hundred sixty thousand and form the largest Indian tribe in North America. In their own language, they are *dine*, "the People."

Their winter dwellings are called *hogans*, one-room houses usually not more than twenty-five feet in diameter. The hogan also occupies a central place in the sacred world of the Navajo, for rituals of curing can only be carried out in the hogan. Temporary shelters, or "shades," are built for summer use by families.

The Navajo practice a combination of sheep husbandry and dry-farming agriculture, but have long valued their sheep perhaps more than any other material objects. The sale of lambs, wool, and pelts produces cash income; the raising of goats also provides meat and milk throughout the year. Herding is a daily activity; every person has experience at it. One Navajo recalled: "When I started with the sheep, that became all my work and all my life."[3]

The Navajo place their highest value on the well-being of the family. The reason for working hard and accumulating wealth is so that " . . . your children will have everything. They won't starve, they won't be ragged, they won't hunger for meat and other things. . . . " Poverty is a powerful and mysterious monster in Navajo mythology and its avoidance is a cardinal goal in Navajo life. "I'm telling you this because I don't want you to be poor," a father regularly advised his son.[4] Another important asset is ceremonial knowledge, considered to be a real object of wealth as well as a form of insurance. One Navajo remarked: "Knowing a good story will protect your home and children and property." Another tells: "Even if you have only one song for the sheep, you'll raise them, nothing will bother them. . . . "[5]

The height of Navajo artistic expression is reached in the most ephemeral of arts—the making of sand paintings, created by pouring patterns of pigmented sand onto a floor. These paintings are a vital aspect of the curing rituals; the patient is instructed to sit on the central figure of the painting during the course of the ceremony. Hours are consumed in their construction, and yet the painting itself has little value when finished and may be obliterated in less than half an hour. Navajo ritual is focused upon restoring the harmony between an individual and other persons or supernatural forces, whereas the basic theme in almost all Pueblo rituals is that of restoring harmony in the whole universe.[6]

VIEW OF NAVAJO CORNFIELD, CANYON DE CHELLY

Canyon de Chelly lies at the heart of the Navajo Indian reservation. To the Navajo, it is the rift in the earth from which the gods emerged to direct and teach men. The echoing walls seem to send back voices from those who no longer walk the earth. The canyon is not only the home of the Navajo gods but of the prehistoric people, the Anasazi, or Ancient Ones, who are ancestral to the Hopi.

Comprised of more than one hundred and thirty-one square miles (over eighty-three thousand acres), the canyon is characterized by dramatic red sandstone walls, within which are more than four hundred ancient Indian cliff dwellings. Hundreds of wall paintings and rock carvings (pictographs and petroglyphs) made by both the Anasazi and the Navajo are to be seen everywhere in the canyon, in caves and on sheltered rock ledges.

CANYON DEL MUERTO, ANTELOPE HOUSE RUIN

Named after a Spanish massacre of 1805, in which a large number of Navajo women and children were killed, Canyon del Muerto forks off to the east from Canyon de Chelly. Antelope House is one of the largest canyon ruins and sits at the base of a cliff. The Navajo still use some of the shallow cave sites as storage rooms for dried peaches and corn.

Canyon de Chelly was inhabited at various times by the Basket Makers, cliff dwellers, Hopi Indians, and the Navajo. Beneath the precipitous rock ledges pictographs and petroglyphs from various periods in time depict animals, hunters, dancers, sheep, and Spaniards on horseback.

Much of Navajo mythology is centered on the various rock formations in the canyon. Spider Rock, for example, which rises eight hundred feet from the canyon floor, is the legendary home of Spider Woman, who, according to myth, taught weaving to the Navajo.

NAVAJO COUPLE IN FRONT OF HOGAN

Hogans are not just dwellings for eating and sleeping; they also occupy a central place in the Navajo's sacred world.

NAVAJO MOTHER AND CHILD

New hogans are often consecrated with blessings such as "let this be assurance that the place will be happy."[7]

NAVAJO INDIAN WEAVER, GANADO, ARIZONA

For more than three hundred years, the Navajo have been excellent weavers, their traditional blankets being exceptional creations. Each blanket was a manifestation of the soul-spirit of the individual weaver. It " . . . was not only a distinctive expression, but a way of presenting its wearer to the world. . . . A blanket presented both the tribe and the individual. . . . It was . . . the dynamic expression of a self-image, and its variety within an established tradition reflected the Navajo's assertive individuality."[8]

No preliminary sketches were ever made and no two blankets were ever alike. Bold color and pattern gave exceptional visual energy to each creation. Unlike the Pueblo weavers, from whom they learned the craft, the Navajo have used their imagination to elaborate upon traditional patterns and designs. Each phase of the weaving process was accompanied by particular songs, and too much time spent at the loom was considered harmful.

YOUNG NAVAJO WITH HERD OF GOATS, WALNUT CANYON, ARIZONA

Flocks of sheep and goats were corralled near the Navajo homes, and much of the herding was done by children. Adult Navajos still herd on horseback. Herding methods reflect a blend of native magical belief and practical wisdom. One middle-aged Navajo talked about his people's methods of livestock care: "Early in the morning we take the sheep out of the corral, I sing a song and open the gate. When the sheep are half out my song is half finished. When they are all out I stop my song. They eat grass all day. They mustn't eat loco weed or they go crazy and run all around. If they eat sagebrush, I mustn't give them water or they will get blown out . . . . Then there is owl-foot weed. If they eat that they throw up and die. When you are out herding there are songs for the protection of the sheep and to make them increase."[9]

NAVAJO MAIDEN, GANADO, ARIZONA

"I have always been a poor man. I do not know a single song," said a Navajo informant to anthropologist W. W. Hill as he began his account of agricultural practices. "It is impossible," observes Dr. Hill, "to state too strongly the belief as illustrated by that statement. It summed up in a few words the whole attitude of the Navajo toward life and the possibility of success. With respect to agriculture, it was not the vicissitudes of the environment that made for successful crops or failures, but the control of the natural forces through ritual." [10]

A NAVAJO SILVERSMITH

The Navajo are renowned as silversmiths. Both men and women wear silver and turquoise belts, bracelets, and beads liberally. The design of Navajo silver ornaments has its roots in the goods that were bartered with English and other colonial settlers as early as 1750. Design was also influenced by Mexican–Spanish bridal trappings and European costume ornamentation of the late eighteenth and early nineteenth centuries. This silversmith is working a piece of silver for the shaping of a bracelet. The forge, an open furnace in which metal is heated before shaping, has been fired and is ready for use. A bellows is barely discernible in the background.

CASA BLANCA, CANYON DE CHELLY

Here is a breathtaking view of the Canyon de Chelly, home of the Navajo, with its sweeping rose-red cliffs: phantoms of natural quiet and of celestial scale. The cliff and canyon-floor dwelling units were once connected to one another. Clearly visible is White House Ruin, one of the earliest homes built by the Anasazi, before A.D. 1200.

CANYON DE CHELLY

The contemporary Kiowa writer N. Scott Momaday spent his childhood growing up among the Navajo. In his memoir, The Names, *he writes: "If you have ever been to the hogans in Canyon de Chelly, or to a squaw dance near Lukachukai—if you have ever heard the riding songs in the dusk, or the music of the yeibichai [a Navajo healing ceremony]—you will never come away entirely, but a part of you will remain there always; you will have found an old home of the spirit."[11] From the folds of the earth, the red walls rise sheer; you are looking into "a corridor of geologic time." You turn a corner and the walls contain you.*

*I HEARD THE SINGING AND DRUMMING AS SOON AS WE REACHED
THE PUEBLO, AND IT DREW ME STRONGLY AND I LEFT THE OTHERS
AND RAN HURRIEDLY TOWARDS IT... ALL OF A SUDDEN I WAS
BROUGHT UP AGAINST THE TRIBE, WHERE A DIFFERENT INSTINCT
RULED, WHERE A DIFFERENT KNOWLEDGE GAVE A DIFFERENT POWER
FROM ANY I HAD KNOWN, AND WHERE VIRTUE LAY IN WHOLENESS
INSTEAD OF IN DISMEMBERMENT.... I FELT A STRONG NEW LIFE WAS
PRESENT THERE ENFOLDING ME.*

MABEL DODGE LUHAN (1917)[1]

THE RIO GRANDE AND WESTERN PUEBLOS

"Taos . . . and the other pueblos . . . have colonized artists and poets of late . . . . At last the wisdom of the ages has . . . made us aware . . . of . . . vivid creations of primitive art. . . ."[1a]

The Pueblo Indians include the Hopi and Zuni tribes in northeastern Arizona and western New Mexico, as well as those of the eastern pueblos—Taos, San Ildefonso, and Isleta—along the Rio Grande River in central New Mexico, and Acoma to the south. Only about thirty pueblos still survive of some seventy that were inhabited at the time Francisco Vásquez de Coronado made contact with them in 1540. Coronado was in search of the "Seven Cities of Cíbola," reputed to be fabulously rich in gold and precious stones. Instead, he found self-sustaining communal units, which he called *pueblos*, the Spanish word for "villages." The native people farmed, raised cotton, and had flocks of turkeys.

Even before the Spaniards arrived, Pueblo territories were growing smaller. Prolonged drought in the thirteenth century brought major changes in the landscape and the river systems. Many villages were abandoned. Inter-pueblo warfare caused the destruction of many more.

Pueblo culture reached its greatest level of development during the fourteenth century, when it extended across vast portions of the southwestern United States. It was during this period that the magnificent villages of the Mesa Verde region, in what is now southwestern Colorado, arrived at their peak. Other remarkable sites included Canyon de Chelly and Kayenta in northeastern Arizona.

As Spanish subjects, under the ruthless and brutal rule of Coronado, the Pueblos suffered abuse and were exploited. Invasion and repeated colonization efforts forced the villages to consolidate and adopt an appearance of acquiescence. Spanish authorities, both civil and ecclesiastical, attempted to destroy native traditional beliefs and sacred rites and replace them with orthodox Catholic beliefs and customs. Seventeenth-century records are replete with instances of attempts to eradicate native ceremonies by force.[2] Pueblo kivas were raided and ceremonial paraphernalia was burned. Indians were forcibly baptized and made to attend Mass. Resistance brought immediate physical punishment, including lashings and imprisonment.

With the arrival of the Anglo–Americans—in particular the missionaries of other religions—native ceremonial rites were once again criticized as "obscene," "immoral," and "idolatrous." Indian children were taken from their families and enrolled in boarding schools, often at considerable distances from the reservations. The intention was to alienate the children from their traditional culture. These acts by missionaries and United States government officials forced the Pueblos to strengthen their native ceremonial practices, though many Indians became completely acculturated.

Today, in the sweeping vastitudes of the Pueblo landscape, which is given dramatic scale by the diminutive adobe buildings nestled close to the earth, Pueblo sacred customs are vigorously renewed, but they are closely guarded—for fear of a time remembered.

THE NOISE OF PASSING FEET
ON THE PRAIRIE—
IS IT MEN OR GODS
WHO CAME OUT OF THE SILENCE?
                    ALICE CORBIN (1920)[3]

RIDERS IN THE WHITE SANDS, NEW MEXICO

In her novel Death Comes for the Archbishop, *Willa Cather described the look and feel of riding across the desert flats in the 1920s: "This mesa plain had an appearance of great antiquity, and of incompleteness; as if, with all the materials for world-making assembled, the Creator had desisted, gone away and left everything on the point of being brought together, on the eve of being arranged into mountain, plain, plateau. The country was still waiting to be made into a landscape."[4]*

TENTS OF OTOWI

Otowi, from the native word Po-tsu-wïï, *or "water sink gap," was a large pueblo of terraced houses constructed of stone and estimated to have contained seven hundred and fifty rooms and ten circular kivas. These monolithic structures are carved out of the tuff formations (volcanic ash deposits) near Los Alamos, New Mexico, in the present-day Bandelier National Monument. Most of the area is covered with thick layers of compacted volcanic ash collectively called "Bandelier tuff." The region is believed to be the prehistoric home of the Tewa Indians of the San Ildefonso pueblo.*

TYUONYI RUINS FROM ABOVE, CANYON OF RITO DE LOS FRIJOLES
(NOW BANDELIER NATIONAL MONUMENT), NEW MEXICO

A huge ancient pueblo, this great circular community was estimated to be three stories high in places and contained some four hundred rooms. It was
discovered in 1890 by historian Adolph Bandelier and Charles F. Lummis, author, naturalist, and ardent advocate of Indian rights. Lummis
observed that "the walls of these ground-floor rooms stand four to eight feet high, and in places there are remnants of another story. The whole ground
plan suggest[s] a gigantic honeycomb."[5] Tree-ring dates from Tyuonyi indicate that much of the construction occurred between A.D. 1383 and 1466.
The people who lived here were farmers; they grew crops of corn, beans, and squash on the floor of the canyon and on the surrounding mesa tops.
Both the Keresan- and Tewa-speaking Pueblos claim this region as their ancestral homeland, and their legends and traditions strongly support their
claim. In the Keresan language, the name Tyuonyi is said to mean "meeting place" or "place of treaty." The Tewa called the ruin Puqwige'onwikeji,
or "old pueblo where the bottoms of the pottery vessels were smoothed thin." For reasons unknown, by the mid-1500s, Frijoles Canyon was
abandoned as a permanent homesite.

THE INDIANS SAY TAOS IS THE HEART OF THE WORLD. THEIR WORLD, MAYBE. SOME PLACES SEEM TEMPORARY ON THE FACE OF THE EARTH: SAN FRANCISCO FOR EXAMPLE. SOME PLACES SEEM FINAL. THEY HAVE A TRUE NODALITY. . . . PLACES CAN LOSE THEIR LIVING NODALITY. ROME, TO ME, HAS LOST HERS. IN VENICE ONE FEELS THE MAGIC OF THE GLAMOROUS OLD NODE THAT ONCE UNITED EAST AND WEST, BUT IT IS THE BEAUTY OF AN AFTERLIFE.

TAOS PUEBLO STILL RETAINS ITS OLD NODALITY. NOT LIKE A GREAT CITY. BUT, IN ITS WAY, LIKE ONE OF THE MONASTERIES OF EUROPE. . . .

TAOS PUEBLO AFFECTS ME LIKE ONE OF THE OLD MONASTERIES. WHEN YOU GET THERE YOU FEEL SOMETHING FINAL. THERE IS AN ARRIVAL. THE NODALITY STILL HOLDS GOOD. . . .

THERE IT IS THEN, THE PUEBLO AS IT HAS BEEN SINCE HEAVEN KNOWS WHEN. AND THE SLOW DARK WEAVING OF THE INDIAN LIFE GOING ON STILL, THOUGH PERHAPS MORE WAVERINGLY. AND ONESELF, SITTING THERE ON A PONY, A FAR-OFF STRANGER WITH GULFS OF TIME BETWEEN ME AND THIS. AND YET, THE OLD NODALITY OF THE PUEBLO STILL HOLDING, LIKE A DARK GANGLION SPINNING INVISIBLE THREADS OF CONSCIOUSNESS. A SENSE OF DRYNESS, ALMOST OF WEARINESS, ABOUT THE PUEBLO. AND A SENSE OF THE INALTERABLE. . . .

D. H. LAWRENCE (1923)[6]

PUEBLO OF TAOS, NORTH SIDE, NEW MEXICO

Taos is the northernmost of all the Rio Grande pueblos and lies about fifty miles north of Santa Fe. It is surrounded completely by the peaks and crags of the Sangre de Cristo mountain range, which imparts a forbidding and sublime element to the landscape. The upper levels of the terraced buildings of Taos pueblo are reached by ladders and stone steps. This section of the pueblo presents an impressive example of urban architecture, rising to a height of seven stories. The upper stories are generally used for living, while the lower levels are relegated to storage. Many of the chimney tops still in use are made from broken pots and shards.

CHILDREN OF TAOS PUEBLO, NEW MEXICO

STREET SCENE, TAOS PUEBLO, NEW MEXICO

*THE SPIRIT OF ADVENTURISM HAS BEEN TRANSLATED INTO A MAGIC
CARPET GUARANTEED TO TAKE ONE "AWAY FROM IT ALL"...LEAV[ING]
THE TRAVELER WITH HIS...MEMORIES OF SUPERFICIAL CONTACT
WITH ROUSSEAU'S "NATURAL MAN." THE LOSSES THAT RESULT FROM
THIS ACCELERATING PROCESS ARE UNRECOVERABLE.*

ALEXANDER ALLAND, JR.
(ANTHROPOLOGIST)[7]

ESTUFA, SAN ILDEFONSO PUEBLO, NEW MEXICO

San Ildefonso has a grand, dusty plaza, yellow with sun. One majestic cottonwood tree still remains in it. The estufa, the kiva of the eastern pueblos, dominates. It is both dwelling and temple, a place where much social and economic activity occurs, but its principal use is for the preparation and performance of ceremonies.

By the 1920s, southwestern motor cruising had become fashionable and the Santa Fe Railway and Fred Harvey offered their transcontinental rail patrons a romantic three-day interlude—an "Indian Detour" through the Indian pueblos and prehistoric cliff dwellings of northern New Mexico. Passengers were met by chauffeurs, couriers, and Packard touring cars at Lamy, Albuquerque, and Winslow and whisked off to the hills to catch their first glimpse of Indians and ruins.

In this picture, the Santa Fe "detourists" have been accompanied to San Ildefonso to view one of the social dances and then purchase some of the famous black pottery ware of the pueblo. The Fred Harvey driver wears his Stetson hat and Western outfit; the Indians have dressed up for the occasion, bedecked in popular Plains-style headdresses.

ZUNI PUEBLO WITH CORN MOUNTAIN IN THE DISTANCE

Corn Mountain, Dowa Yalanne in the Zuni language, looms a thousand feet above the sun-drenched plain of western New Mexico and dominates the life of the Zuni people. It is the location of important and sacred shrines to which the Zuni make pilgrimages throughout the year. Zuni is surrounded by sandy flats. When the artist William R. Leigh visited Zuni in 1906, he found it marvelously picturesque, "all rose pink." In a letter, he wrote: "When I took my paint box and went to the town the experience was more like a waking dream than actuality. Here was the town, the people, whom Coronado had known. This was the town which had been reported to be paved and roofed with gold. . . . The women wore red blankets which contrasted marvelously with their black hair. It seemed as if it would be impossible to add or take away anything to heighten the fabulous picturesqueness. Color, line, massing, distribution, everything was perfect. The people made wonderful pottery and unique jewelry. They wove beautiful girdles and other handwoven garments."[8]

A PUEBLO HOME

The traditional straw-roofed sunbreak, or ramada, supported by the frame shown in front of this house, was used both as a drying rack for vegetables, fruits, meats, and animal skins and for storing wood. This outdoor living space was used for cooking, eating, and visiting; sometimes a baby's cradle was suspended from the rafters. The colorful ristratas of chili drying on the wall and on the ground were a staple in Pueblo cooking.

The availability of glass was a great boon, and it was incorporated immediately into pueblo house building.

THE CHILD IS A PERSON WHO HAS JUST COME FROM THE GREAT MYSTERIOUS, AND I WHO AM AN OLD MAN AM ABOUT TO RETURN TO THE GREAT MYSTERY. AND SO IN REALITY WE ARE VERY CLOSE TO EACH OTHER.

AN OLD LAKOTA INDIAN[9]

LAGUNA PUEBLO, MOTHER AND CHILD

From the first day of its life, the newborn Pueblo infant is bound to a cradle board, a flat plank with a wicker bow, which acts as a guard for the baby's head, arching over one end. The baby is secured to the board by strips of cloth or strings laced through holes at its sides. Often a cloth canopy is fastened to the arch to protect the baby's face from the sun. Except for bathing and the changing of clothing, the infant generally spends its first three to six months almost exclusively on the cradle board. Even nursing takes place there. The use of the cradle board is regarded as an assurance of good carriage and straightness in a child. It is also believed to contribute to the infant's feeling of security. Confinement in the cradle has no known effect on motor development.

WATCH YOUR STEP! NAVAJO WEAVING DANCE, TESUQUE PUEBLO

LAGUNA. IN SOAK. THE BATHING POOL

RIO GRANDE PUEBLO WOMEN AT WORK

Women's activities center in home, which they own and usually occupy throughout their lives. As in most pueblos, the women share heavily in the task of house building and maintenance. They do the plastering and finishing, while the men assist in the laying of stones and the placement of wooden beams. "The house is always built in the form of a parallelogram," writes the anthropologist Victor Mindeleff, "the walls being from seven to eight feet high and of irregular thickness . . . . Pine, piñon, juniper, cottonwood . . . indeed all the available trees of the region are used in house construction."[10]

WOOD GATHERER

Since there was hardly a growing thing in the immediate pueblo surroundings worth collecting for fuel, wood gathering took the men to distant mesas. "Fuel seemed hardest to get and fastest to go," recorded Sun Chief in his journal. "Old men and women, some nearly blind, would go far out into the plains and return with bundles of brush and sticks on their backs. Whenever my father herded, he spent his spare time breaking dead bushes of juniper or greasewood, leaving them in little piles to be brought into the village on burros."[11]

BAKING BREAD: SAN ILDEFONSO PUEBLO. NEW MEXICO

In 1582 Antonio de Espejo, an early Spanish explorer, described his entry into the Rio Grande pueblos: "The inhabitants of each town came out to meet us, took us to their pueblos, and gave us quantities of turkeys, corn, beans and tortillas, with other kinds of bread, which they make more skillfully than the Mexican people. They grind raw corn on very large stones, five or six women working together in a single mill, and from the flour they make many kinds of bread."[12]

The oven, built of stones, plastered inside and out, has a small vent at the top and an opening at the base for the insertion of fuel as well as dough. A variety of fuels was used: corncobs, sheep dung, and wood. Loaves were inserted into the oven with a long-handled paddle, shown at the bottom edge of the smoke.

PUEBLO WOMAN GRINDING CORNMEAL

"Corn is life, and piki is the perfect food," relates a common Hopi saying. The Hopi have an extensive vocabulary for corn in their language, which includes words for parts of the plant that are unknown to Anglo–American culture. Fifty-two varieties of corn foods can easily be counted. Piki, a paper-thin corn wafer, is the most popular. With a swift movement of the hand, the thin batter is spread over a smoothly polished, heated stone, the result being a very fine leaflike sheet of bread. Plant blossoms are sometimes added to the batter to produce color and add to the flavor.

To be without corn was a calamity. Every household tried to keep a full year's supply of corn on hand, and it was used sparingly. Hopi corn is grown in an astonishing variety of colors—white, yellow, red, blue, and purple, which the Hopi call black, as well as mottled.[13]

TURQUOISE DRILLER, ZUNI

The Zuni learned the art of silversmithing and turquoise setting from the Navajo, and today they are considered to be the leading Pueblo jewelers. Lanyade was the first native in Zuni pueblo to learn the craft: "When I was young, about thirty years old [1872], a Navajo came to Zuni who knew how to make silver. . . . We became good friends . . . and he came over to my house and lived. At that time no one in Zuni knew how to make silver, and we had never seen anyone make it. We had seen the Mexicans and the Navajo wearing it and we had bought some pieces of it from them. But those silver buttons and bracelets were very expensive, and only a few people in the village had any. . . . I told him [Atsidi Chon] that I would give him a good horse if he would teach me how to work with the silver. So he taught me how, and I was the only Zuni to learn from him."[14] In the picture, the driller is boring a hole in the center of a turquoise bead with a drill pump "made to revolve by a pumping motion with the crosspiece, while the flywheel produces rotation which unwinds the thongs in one direction and rewinds them in the other. . . ."[15]

I AM A MEDICINE MAN BECAUSE A DREAM TOLD ME TO BE ONE, BE-CAUSE I AM COMMANDED TO BE ONE, BECAUSE THE OLD HOLY MEN —CHEST, THUNDERHAWK, CHIPS, GOOD LANCE—HELPED ME TO BE ONE.... YOU BECOME A PEJUTA WICASA, A MEDICINE MAN AND HEALER, BECAUSE A DREAM TELLS YOU TO DO THIS. NO ONE MAN DREAMS OF ALL THE MEDICINES. YOU DOCTOR WHERE YOU KNOW YOU HAVE THE POWER. YOU DON'T INHERIT IT; YOU WORK FOR IT, FAST FOR IT, TRY TO DREAM IT UP, BUT IT DOESN'T ALWAYS COME. IT IS TRUE THAT SOME FAMILIES PRODUCE A STRING OF GOOD MEDI-CINE MEN, AND IT HELPS TO HAVE A HOLY MAN AMONG YOUR RELA-TIVES WHO TEACHES YOU AND TRIES TO PASS HIS POWER ON TO YOU. IT WORKS SOMETIMES, BUT NOT ALWAYS. MEDICINE MEN AREN'T HORSES. YOU DON'T BREED THEM.... SEEING ME IN MY PATCHED-UP, FADED SHIRT, WITH MY DOWN-AT-THE-HEELS COWBOY BOOTS...IT ALL DOESN'T ADD UP TO A WHITE MAN'S IDEA OF A HOLY MAN.... BUT I'VE BEEN UP ON THE HILLTOP, GOT MY VISION AND MY POWER, THE REST IS JUST TRIMMINGS. THAT VISION NEVER LEAVES ME....

LAME DEER (MEDICINE MAN)[16]

MEDICINE MAN, TESUQUE, NEW MEXICO

The medicine man "keeps the universe moving," insuring reciprocity between man and nature. He is the keeper of the "old time ways, the tribal rituals and stories, as well as guardian of the spirit and morale which lie at the center of pueblo life." Priest, magician, medicine man, shaman—all are native healers whose mystical practices include visions, fasting, singing, drumming, and the shaking of rattles. They are believed to hold within their power both prosperity and adversity. Their art goes back to prehistory. Most important is the power to cure, for disease is seen to be caused by evil spirits and the healer's power enables him to drive these spirits out of the body of the patient. Treatment begins when the medicine man prepares his trance: ". . . he drums, summons his spirit helpers, speaks a 'secret language' or the 'animal language' imitating the cries of beasts and especially the songs of birds."[17] He ends by obtaining a state of ecstasy, of religious inspiration, for medicine men are the keepers of "the secrets of the earth spirit."

ENTERING THE KIVA, RIO GRANDE PUEBLO

INSIDE KIVA SHOWING PRAYER ALTAR, NAMBÉ PUEBLO

DEER DANCE AT TESUQUE PUEBLO, NEW MEXICO

Pueblo animal dances—representing buffalo, elk, antelope, deer, and mountain sheep—are concerned with the perpetuation of the large game animals that were a staple in the Pueblo diet. As many as fifty dancers may assemble for the Deer Dance, or penshare, which is performed in winter as a prophecy of a new season and supplication for new growth. It is believed that its performance ensures an abundant new year. The sticks held by the dancers represent the front legs of the deer; the headdresses consist of deer antlers mounted on "tiaras" of yucca stalks, with turkey feathers tied to each tip. The "deer" make a striking sight, with their stark white shirts, leggings, and darkened faces, as they sing and circle the plaza in pairs. In imitation of the deer, each dancer leans forward and partially supports his weight in different postures on short canes, one in each hand, to imitate the movement of the forefeet of the animal when running or leaping.[18]

CLOSE-UP OF DEER DANCERS AT TESUQUE PUEBLO

In Pueblo symbolism, the six directions (north, south, east, west, above, and below) are associated with specific animals and birds, some of which appear in ritual and dance. For example, the mountain lion, or pingxeng, represents the north. He is identified with the hunt chief, the master of the animals, who leads the Deer Dance. "By impersonating the animal he wished to kill, a hunter could come very close to a herd without being observed. By performing a dance before the hunt, the hunt group believed that they could please the spirits of the animals, which would then permit their earthly bodies to be killed."[19] In dance, the Deer spirits come forth from the mountains and forests and enter the pueblo at dawn. Antelope, mountain sheep, and elk are now scarce, but their presence continues through impersonation—in animal heads, pelts, masks, and elaborate costumes. Their horns and hoofs decorate the headdresses and knee rattles of the impersonators. The dancers shake the earth ". . . describ[ing] every impulse, the whole rhythm of the turning of the earth, the returning of time upon it forever."[20]

INDIAN CEREMONIAL DANCE—THE BASKET DANCE

This solemn and beautiful dance, marked by the slow rhythmic swaying of the participants, promotes fertility in all realms of life through the symbolic power of the baskets carried by the women. The invocations for fertility touch upon not only food but also the human race, which must multiply and transmit the gift of life from generation to generation. The scenes dramatized in the ritual express the entire scope of a woman's life, her dedication to child rearing and thus the sustaining of life in the pueblo.

FIESTA DAY AT TAOS, NEW MEXICO

On Fiesta Day each pueblo celebrates its patron saint. The fiesta combines Catholic elements—a Mass and a procession of the saint's image, which is carried into the plaza—combined with native ritual dancing. N. Scott Momaday recalls with delight his experience of a Fiesta Day: "Jemez [pueblo] became one of the fabulous cities of the world. In the preceding days the women had plastered the houses . . . they were clean and beautiful like bone in the high light . . . ears of colored corn were strung at the doors, and fresh cedar boughs were laid about, setting a whole, wild fragrance on the air. . . ."[21]

WAR DANCE, ZUNI PUEBLO, NEW MEXICO

The dance recalls memories of Navajo raids. In it, the war whoop and a response precede each song. Some of the Zuni men imitate Navajos; others hold arrows, handling them in a way to suggest the death of the enemy. Some dancers assume attitudes of attack; others, of defense; one poses in the act of drawing a bow, another swings a war club, and some act as if they are throwing a tomahawk. The dance is a symbolic expression of the Zunis' defense of their cornfields from marauding Navajo.[22] The dance celebrates Zuni identity as a Pueblo people with a different way of life, and their strong sense of this identity is what has kept the ritual alive.

A CORN DANCER, RIO GRANDE PUEBLO

The Corn Dance, xoxeye, is an important ripening ceremony and a deep plea for the rain clouds to weep bounteously. The critical element in this enactment is the interplay between the dancers' emotions, the seasons, and all aspects of the natural environment. In this picture the dancer holds a gourd rattle in his left hand. When in motion, its impelling gesture is meant to lure rain. The dancer is decked in spruce boughs and carries a spruce "lance" as well. These ritual objects are invested with the power to bring rain and enhance fertility. The ritual itself brings order and purpose to life, and when performed to the best of the dancer's ability, the Pueblo Indian knows, in the words of John Collier, "that he is raised into vastness, made free from personal trouble, flooded with impersonal joy and ardor, and plunged into the ever-flowing tide of the tribal world soul."[24]

INDIAN CORN DANCE AT SANTA CLARA, NEW MEXICO

Corn is the very life of the pueblo, and all Rio Grande Pueblos perform the Corn Dance, usually on the name day of the saint for whom the Spaniards named their village. The entire ceremony is a calling-out for the roar of rain. The dancers urge the fields to yield, reminding all that life is strong. The dance is graceful beyond measure, with as many as two hundred dancers participating. The whole plaza becomes a magnificent spectacle, a "sea of evergreen and cloud altars," as the dancers sweep around it in labyrinthine patterns, moving to the rise and fall of chanting and the beating of drums.[25]

BLESSING OF THE CORN CEREMONY, RIO GRANDE PUEBLO

Nothing could be more sculptural and pictorial in the Pueblo world than the beautiful formations of the Corn Dance. Art and religion unite here in a tremendous display of color and geometric pattern, expressing the mind of spring.

The origin of the dance ritual lies deep in Pueblo legend. When Iatiku, a manifestation of the Pueblo Earth Mother, promised her children the gift of corn at the time of their emergence from the Underworld, she said: "Take this corn. It is my heart. It shall be to you as milk from my breasts."[26] Indeed, upon initiation into a men's society, every Hopi youth receives a special ear of corn, which he thereafter refers to as "my mother" because "the Hopi say that the people draw life from corn as the child does from its mother."[27]

THE CORN DANCE, RIO GRANDE PUEBLO, NEW MEXICO

A Pueblo farmer speaks about the importance of the cornfields in his people's life: "This is what we do. This is a part of our lives. We sing to the younger corn telling them to hurry up and catch up with the taller ones, because they are way ahead of them. We think of our cornfields, of our crops and we don't neglect them. We keep encouraging the plants by singing to them so they'll grow faster and so that we'll have plenty for the kids to eat, and for all the people."[28] The Corn Dance is also referred to as the Tablita Dance and the Harvest Dance. In the photograph the women wear the tablita ("little board" in Spanish) upon their heads—one of the distinguishing features of the dance. Mesa and cloud shapes are cut into the tops of the boards to compel the rain to come.

CORN DANCE, SANTA CLARA PUEBLO, NEW MEXICO

Like all Indian dances, the Corn Dance is an "expression of that original human impulse toward the creation of beauty which modern civilization does so much to defeat and destroy."[29] It presents a stunning orchestration of color, song, and movement that resonates delicately with the earth's rhythms and the seasons' cycles. In its supplication for grace, it reaffirms the sanctity of all living things. A sacred drama as well as a celebration of form, it is also a reflection of and response to the natural environment. Joyful shadows pass swiftly over the dancing participants as they exult in their desire for communion. In this commonality of oneness and "through [the ceremony's] perfect . . . enactment . . . the tribe commingled with the universe and contributed . . . meaning and power."[30]

NOTES AND REFERENCES

1. Quoted in Stewart L. Udall, *The Quiet Crisis* (New York: Holt, Rinehart and Winston, 1963), 3.

2. Quoted in Maria F. Mahoney, *The Meaning of Dreams and Dreaming* (Secaucus, N.J.: The Citadel Press, 1966), 240.

3. Quoted in Gilbert Harrison, ed., *Gertrude Stein's America* (Washington, D. C.: Robert B. Luce, 1965), 48.

4. Perry Miller, *Nature's Nation* (Cambridge, Mass.: Harvard University, the Belknap Press, 1967), xv. Miller was convinced that to be an American was "a complex fate," as Henry James had said. It was, in Miller's view, an amazing experience. "Being an American," he said, "is not something inherited but something to be achieved," and, he continued, "he who endeavors to fix the personality of America in one eternal, unchangeable pattern not only understands nothing of how a personality is created, but comprehends little of how this nation has come along thus far." (*Nature's Nation*, Introduction by Kenneth B. Murdock, xiv, xv.)

INTRODUCTION

1. William Webb and Robert A. Weinstein, *Dwellers at the Source* (New York: Grossman Publishers, 1973), 89.

2. John Collier, *Indians of the Americas: The Long Hope* (New York: The New American Library, Mentor Books, 1947), 7.

3. Quoted in Amy Clampitt, *The Kingfisher* (New York: Alfred A. Knopf, 1983), 62. (For a variation in translation, see *Mandelstam: The Complete Critical Prose and Letters*, ed. Jane Gary Harris, trans. Jane Gary Harris and Constance Link [Ann Arbor, Mich.: Ardis, 1979], 113.)

4. Based on original dialogue from Samuel Taylor, *Sabrina Fair: A Comedy in Four Acts* (New York: Dramatists Play Service, 1955), 58.

CORPORATE IMAGE MAKING AND PRIMITIVE CULTURE

Railway Culture: A Call to a New Patriotism

1. Arthur S. Link, David W. Hirst, and John E. Little et al., eds., *The Papers of Woodrow Wilson*, 54 vols. to date (Princeton, N.J.: Princeton University Press, 1966–), 42:74.

2. Flann O'Brien, *The Third Policeman* (London: Pan Books, Picador Edition, 1974), 134.

3. See Robert S. Berkhofer, *The White Man's Indian* (New York: Vintage Books, 1979).

4. Herman Melville, *Billy Budd, Sailor and Other Stories* (Harmondsworth, England: Penguin Books, Penguin English Library, 1967), 105.

5. Walt Whitman, *Specimen Days & Collect* (Philadelphia: Rees Welsh and Company, 1882–83), 139.

6. "Poem XLIII," in *Poems by Emily Dickinson*, ed. Martha Dickinson Bianchi and Alfred Leete Hampson (Boston: Little, Brown, 1952), 22.

7. Ralph Waldo Emerson, *Journals and Miscellaneous Notebooks*, ed. Alfred R. Ferguson et al. 14 vols. (Cambridge, Mass.: Harvard University Press, 1964), 8:335.

8. Quoted in Barbara Novak, *Nature and Culture: American Landscape and Painting, 1825–1875* (New York: Oxford University Press, 1980), 169.

9. Hart Crane, *The Bridge* (New York: Liveright, 1930), 25–26.

10. Thomas Wolfe, "From Death to Morning," in *The Portable Thomas Wolfe* (New York: The Viking Press, 1946), 656.

11. Charles Dickens, "Mugby Junction," in *Christmas Stories* (London: MacDonald and Sons, 1866), pt. 2, 147.

12. Paul Verlaine, "La Bonne Chanson," in *Oeuvres Poétiques*

Completes (Paris, 1951), 106. English translation, by Gertrude Hall, in *Baudelaire, Rimbaud, Verlaine: Selected Verse and Prose Poems* (New York: Citadel Press, 1947), 47.

13. Quoted in Marc Baroli, *Le Train dans la Littérature Française* (Ph.D. diss., Faculté des Lettres et Sciences Humaines de l'Université de Paris, 1964), 58. English translation, by Wolfgang Schivelbusch, in *The Railway Journey* (New York: Urizen Books, 1979), 59. Hugo's position on the advent of the railroad moved from one of strong antipathy ("c'est fort laid") to one of mild acceptance, as demonstrated here.

Wilderness and the American Spirit

1. Henry David Thoreau, "Walking," in *Excursions* (New York: Corinth Books, 1962), 185. (Originally published in 1863.) Thoreau was one of our first preservationists. In 1858, more than a decade before Congress set aside Yellowstone as the first national park, Henry David Thoreau made a plea for "national preserves, in which the bear, and the panther, and some even of the hunter race may still exist, and not be civilized off the face of the earth—not for idle sport or food, but for inspiration and our own true recreation." (Quoted in Udall, *The Quiet Crisis*, 51.)

2. Edgar Allan Poe, "The Elk," in *The Works of Edgar Allan Poe*, 10 vols. (New York: Scribner, 1914), 2:77–78. Cited in Hans Huth, *Nature and the American: Three Centuries of Changing Attitudes* (Berkeley and Los Angeles: University of California Press, 1957; Lincoln: University of Nebraska Press, 1972), 52.

3. W. B. Yeats, "Emotion of Multitude," in *Essays and Introductions* (New York: Macmillan, 1961), 215.

4. Quoted in David M. Steele, *Going Abroad Overland: Studies of Places and People in the Far West* (New York and London: G. P. Putnam's Sons, The Knickerbocker Press, 1917), 38.

5. Pierre M. Irving, *The Life and Letters of Washington Irving*, 3 vols. (New York, G. P. Putnam's Sons, 1873), 1:13–14. (Cited in Huth, *Nature and the American*, 37.)

6. Quoted in Huth, *Nature and the American*, 29.

7. Any comments on the cultural significance of the railroads find their origins in *The Machine in the Garden*, Leo Marx's pioneering work on the nineteenth-century's most ruthless emblem of power. See also Novak, "Man's Traces: Axe, Train, Figure," chap. 8 in *Nature and Culture*.

8. Archibald MacLeish, "Wildwest," in *Collected Poems, 1917–1952* (Boston: Houghton Mifflin, 1952), 70.

9. Gifford Pinchot, *Breaking New Ground* (New York: Harcourt, Brace, 1947), 23.

10. Daniel Davis writes in *The Book of the Telegraph* that the telegraph was originally developed "to regulate railroad traffic [but] differentiated itself as an independent means of communication toward the middle of the 19th century. However, the railroad line and the telegraph usually continued to exist side by side, one keeping the other company, the telegraph wires 'dancing' before the traveller's eyes." (Daniel Davis, *Book of the Telegraph*, published by Daniel Davis, 428 Washington Street, Boston, 1851.) The year of the establishment of the commercial telegraph in America, 1844, was also the year Kierkegaard published "The Concept of Dread."

11. Quoted in Brian O'Doherty, *American Masters* (New York: E. P. Dutton, 1972), 33.

12. Quoted in T. C. McLuhan, *Touch the Earth* (New York: Outerbridge and Dienstfrey, 1971), 15. The Wintu Indians of California lived on very densely wooded land where it was difficult to find clear land even to erect houses. "Nevertheless," wrote anthropologist Dorothy Lee, "they would use only dead wood for fuel out of respect for nature." The entirety of the following passage eloquently reflects the old Wintu's concern about the needless destruction of the land in which she lived, a place where gold mining —particularly hydraulic mining—had torn up the earth.

The White people never cared for land or deer or bear. When we Indians kill meat, we eat it all up. When we dig roots we make little holes. When we build houses, we make little holes. When we burn grass for grasshoppers, we don't ruin things. We shake down acorns and pinenuts. We don't chop down the trees. We only use dead wood. But the White people plow up the ground, pull down the trees, kill everything. The tree says, "Don't. I am sore. Don't hurt me." But they chop it down and cut it up. The spirit of the land hates them. They blast out trees and stir it up to its depths. They saw up the trees. That hurts them. The

Indians never hurt anything, but the White people destroy all. They blast rocks and scatter them on the ground. The rock says, "Don't. You are hurting me." But the White people pay no attention. When the Indians use rocks, they take little round ones for their cooking. . . . How can the spirit of the earth like the White man? . . . Everywhere the White man has touched it, it is sore.

13. Baudelaire was one of the first to write about this state of dis-ease wrought by the industrial order, describing the new urban crowds as being " . . . like errant homeless ghosts doggedly bemoaning." Many began to look for a reaffirmation of the sacredness of life. (Quoted in John Berger, *And Our Faces, My Heart, Brief As Photos* [New York: Pantheon Books, 1984], 63.)

14. Robert Browning, *"Home Thoughts from Abroad,"* Stanza 2, in *The New Oxford Book of English Verse, 1250–1950,* chosen and ed. Helen Gardner (New York and Oxford: Oxford University Press, 1972), 661.

The Santa Fe Railway: Emergence of the New Image Makers

1. Ralph Waldo Emerson, "The Young American," in *Nature, Addresses and Lectures* (Boston and New York: Houghton Mifflin, 1903), 364.

2. "The Santa Fe Railroad was also a vigorous advertiser for the city. F. G. Gurley, President of the Santa Fe, later remarked: 'The commerce of New Mexico's capital influenced the organization of our railroad and from the capital we derived our name.' " (Marta Weigle and Kyle Fiore, *Santa Fe and Taos: The Writer's Era, 1916–1941* [Santa Fe: Ancient City Press, 1982], 15.)

3. William DeHertburn Washington, *Progress and Prosperity* (New York: The National Educational Publishing Company, 1911).

4. Arrell Morgan Gibson, *A Visual Feast* (Chicago: Santa Fe Railway, 1983). Exhibition catalogue of the Santa Fe Railway Company Collection of Southwestern Art.

5. Albert Bigelow Paine, *Mark Twain's Letters*, 2 vols. (New York and London: Harper and Brothers Publishers, 1917), 1:54.

6. Quoted in *The Santa Fe Magazine* 27, no. 8 (July, 1933):44.

7. Edward Hungerford, "A Study in Consistent Railroad Advertising," *The Santa Fe Magazine* 17, no. 4 (March, 1933):45.

8. Charles F. Lummis, "The Artists' Paradise II," *Out West* 29 (September, 1908):191.

9. Quoted in Robert Taft, *Artists and Illustrations of the Old West, 1850–1900* (New York: Charles Scribner's Sons, 1953), 242.

10. Quoted in *American Heritage* 27, no. 2 (February, 1976): 59. For an illuminating discussion of corporate sponsorship by the Santa Fe Railway of the Santa Fe and Taos artists at the turn of the century, see Keith L. Bryant, Jr., "The Atchison, Topeka and Santa Fe Railway and the Development of the Santa Fe and Taos Art Colonies," in *The Western Historical Quarterly* (October, 1978).

11. With the announcement of a new "extra fast, extra fine, extra fare," all-Pullman train, the *Chief*, on November 14, 1926, the Atchison, Topeka and Santa Fe Railway doubled its efforts at "snob appeal," and "Chiefing it" became *the* way to reach Los Angeles. In 1928, writes historian Keith L. Bryant, "new buffet/library cars and diners were added, with the former carrying names such as 'Santanta,' 'Old Wolf,' and 'Geronimo.' " In 1936 the *Super Chief* was introduced and instantly became "the darling" of the ATSF. It was christened by Mrs. Eddie Cantor, her daughters, and actress Eleanor Powell. The *Super Chief* was decked out in Indian motifs—with Southwest colors and Indian names for the cars. "The sleepers," continues Bryant, [were called] "'Isleta,' 'Taos,' 'Oraibi' and 'Laguna.' . . . The observation-sleeper 'Navajo' carried out the Indian motif with turquoise ceiling, goatskin lampshades, sand paintings encased in glass, and upholstery based on Navajo designs." Once again, to have "Chiefed" West was the only way to travel. (Keith L. Bryant, Jr., *History of the Atchison, Topeka and Santa Fe Railway* [New York: Macmillan, 1974], 334, 339, 340–42.)

12. Some examples of that *Zeitgeist* follow. A Santa Fe "engineman" reminisces about the life he devoted entirely to the care and running of a locomotive: "When I started railroading, the engine cab was to me as fairyland, a sort of sacred and mysterious place to be entered with awe . . . . There is a charm about it, of working in all kinds of

194

weather, of moving along under the stars and beholding the beauties of the night, of gliding past farmhouses and fields bathed in the moonlight or seeing meteors flash across the sky, of working in stormy weather when the wind and rain cut your face like knives if you put your head out of the cab, once in a while catching the roar of the exhaust above the sound of the storm, while the lightning flashes and the thunder rolls. And we have fog, too, when you cannot see more than two car lengths ahead, and the word 'if' is ever present in your mind." ("Impressions of an Engineman," *The Santa Fe Magazine* 2, no. 2 [January, 1908]:93–94.)

Noted French anthropologist Claude Lévi-Strauss expressed a similar romanticism in his description of one of his first encounters with Indian culture: " . . . a magic place where the dreams of childhood hold a rendezvous, where century-old tree trunks sing and speak, where indefinable objects watch out for the visitor with the anxious stare of human faces, where animals of superhuman gentleness join their little paws like hands in prayer for the privilege of building the palace of the beaver for the chosen one, of guiding him to the realm of the seals, or of teaching him, with a mystic kiss, the language of the frog or the kingfisher." (Quoted in Allen Wardwell, *Objects of Bright Pride*, 32. Exhibition Catalogue. Published by the Center for Inter-American Relations and the American Federation of Arts, distributed by the University of Washington Press, 1978.)

13. Quoted in Hungerford, "A Study in Consistent Railroad Advertising," 47.

The Calendar Art of the Santa Fe Railway

1. Quoted in Weigle and Fiore, *Santa Fe and Taos*, 17.
2. Quoted in Huth, *Nature and the American*, 187.
3. Quoted in Keith L. Bryant, Jr., "The Origins and Development of the Santa Fe Railway Collection of Western Art," in *Standing Rainbows*. Exhibition catalogue, 1981.
4. Quoted in Van Deren Coke, *Taos and Santa Fe: The Artist's Environment, 1882–1942* (Albuquerque: University of New Mexico Press for the Amon Carter Museum of Western Art, 1963), 25.
5. Quoted in Arrell Morgan Gibson, *The Santa Fe and Taos Colonies: Age of the Muses, 1900–1942* (Norman: University of Oklahoma Press, 1983), 23.
6. Quoted in Kay Aiken Reeve, *The Making of an American Place: The Development of Santa Fe and Taos, New Mexico, as an American Cultural Center, 1898–1942* (Ph.D. diss., Texas A & M University, 1977), 145.
7. Quoted in Coke, *Taos and Santa Fe*, 17.
8. Quoted in Fred S. Bartlett, *Walt Kuhn* (The Amon Carter Museum of Western Art and the Colorado Springs Fine Arts Center, 1964). Exhibition catalogue.
9. Quoted in Coke, *Taos and Santa Fe*, 32.
10. Quoted in Gibson, *The Santa Fe and Taos Colonies*, 23.
11. Quoted in Coke, *Taos and Santa Fe*, 34.
12. Simpson's poetry was known and appreciated by the artists of Santa Fe and Taos. The following "Hopi Love Songs or You" is excerpted from Simpson's popular volume, which was published in 1929, a few years before his death. *(Along Old Trails: Poems of New Mexico and Arizona* [Boston and New York: Houghton Mifflin, 1929], 37.)

Was it a flute
At the spring
I heard?
Or moccasined winds
On the foot-trail
I heard?
Or you,
In my wonder-dream calling?

13. Coke, *Taos and Santa Fe*, 59.
14. Atchison, Topeka and Santa Fe Railway files, correspondence, Simpson to Couse, March 17, 1925.
15. Ibid., January 29, 1925.
16. Ibid., November 19, 1931.
17. Ibid., February 10, 1927.
18. Ibid., November 19, 1931.
19. Ibid., Couse to Simpson, December 14, 1931.
20. Ibid., Simpson to Couse, February 10, 1927.
21. Quoted in Coke, *Taos and Santa Fe*, 61.
22. Quoted in Gibson, *The Santa Fe and Taos Colonies*, 57.

The Great American Amalgam: Technology and Culture

1. Berger, *And Our Faces, My Heart, Brief As Photos*, 87.
2. Quoted in Susan Sontag, *On Photography* (New York: Dell Publishing Company, 1973), 207.

3. Quoted in Beaumont Newhall and Diana E. Edkins, *William H. Jackson* (New York and Fort Worth: Morgan and Morgan, and the Amon Carter Museum of Western Art, 1974), 136.

4. Ibid., 136. In 1902 an article in *Photo-Miniature* magazine reported that "the duties of a railroad photographer [were] legion,—embracing the photographing of bridges, culverts, stations, signal-cabins, train sheds, sidings and the general equipment of the road. Apart from this comes emergency work. When an accident occurs the photographer is rushed to the spot, and photographs are made from every point for the use of the road officials, or in court . . . .

   "Passenger roads also need photographs showing the scenic attractions along their lines. This calls for landscape work comprising sections of the road itself and picturesque places, pleasure resorts, fruit orchards and farms, mining and industrial plants, views of the towns through which the road passes and other scenes readily accessible from the line which may have interest to the traveler." (*Photo-Miniature* 4 [April, 1902–March, 1903]: 565.)

5. Ibid., 146.

6. Ibid., 136.

7. Ibid., 21.

8. Ibid., 148.

9. Ibid., 149.

10. Mrs. E. H. Kemp, "Photographers in the Hopi Land," *Camera Craft Magazine* 2 (1905): 247.

11. Quoted in Hungerford, "A Study in Consistent Railroad Advertising," 44.

12. *The Santa Fe Magazine* 11, no. 1 (December, 1916): 47.

13. "Eating Houses in Hard Luck," *The Santa Fe Magazine* 1, no. 2 (January, 1907): 51. The indiscriminate practice of collecting "snapshots" provoked the astute social observer Samuel Butler to deplore the fact that "there [was] a photographer in every bush, going about like a roaring lion seeking whom he may devour." But whatever the snapshot lacked in aesthetic quality, it more than made up for through the curiosity it provoked about faraway places amongst friends and relatives of returning travelers.

   The principle of the souvenir snapshot was, however, established long before the appearance of the camera, noted John Turner and Louis Ash in *The Golden Hordes:*

International Tourism and the Pleasure Periphery (London: Constable, 1975). "The [eighteenth-century] Grand Tourist in Rome would pose to have his portrait painted against a backdrop of a suitable high cultural tone, the Colosseum or the Forum and a scattering of atmospheric cypresses. As can be imagined the Roman souvenir portrait developed into a minor industry, providing a useful source of income not only for local artists but also for foreign artists who had come to Rome to study the glories of antiquity at first hand." (Turner and Ash, *The Golden Hordes*, 40.)

The Age of the Magic Lantern

1. D. H. Lawrence, "New Mexico," in *Phoenix I: The Posthumous Papers of D. H. Lawrence*, ed. Edward D. McDonald (London: William Heinemann, 1936; New York: The Viking Press, 1939), 141.

2. Quoted in Pierre Schneider, *Matisse* (Rizzoli International Publications, 1984), 209.

3. The theatrical spectacle of optical-projection systems goes back at least three hundred years. Its origins and invention are popularly attributed to a German-born Jesuit priest, Athanasius Kircher, who taught at the Collegio Romano and who invented, among other things, an ear trumpet and a rudimentary calculator. In 1646, in his book entitled *Ars Magna Lucis et Umbrae*, Kircher describes a form of lantern. The magic lantern wasn't given public currency, however, until the 1790s. Until then, it was limited to very small audiences because of its very weak light source. The problem was rectified by improvements in wicks and reflectors that gave rise to brighter oil lamps. (Robert Eskind, *Magic Lantern: From Rome to Manchester*, unpublished paper, April 28, 1978.)

4. An old dictionary defined the magic lantern as "a small optical instrument which shows by a gloomy light on a wall monsters so hideous that those who are ignorant of the secret believe it to be performed by magic!" Magic indeed. While the public may have seen drawings of monsters, they had never seen the kinds of luminous and free-standing images projected by a magic lantern. (*The Optical Magic Lantern Journal and Photographic Enlarger, June, 1889–May, 1890*, vol. 1, no. 2 (July 15, 1889): 16.

5. Robert Eskind, "Transparent Transformations," *Exposure* 21, no. 2 (1983): 16.

6. *The Optical Magic Lantern Journal and Photographic Enlarger, June, 1889–May, 1890*, vol. 2, no. 28 (September 1, 1891), notes.

7. Eskind, "Transparent Transformations," 17.

8. *The Optical Magic Lantern Journal and Photographic Enlarger, June, 1889–May, 1890*, vol. 1, no. 6 (November 15, 1889): 46.

9. The inventors of photography were keenly aware of the limitations of the black-and-white photographic image. In 1816 Joseph Nicephore Niépce wrote: "I need to arrive at some way of fixing the color, that is what is concerning me at the moment, and it is the thing which is the most difficult. Without that it would not be worth anything." It was not until the invention of the autochrome process at the beginning of the twentieth century that color photography was possible. Technical complexities and the high cost of production, however, limited the use of this process. These problems remained unsolved for decades until new developments in photochemistry provided a basis for making inexpensive color film that provided true colors. (Cited in Adrian Bailey and Adrian Holloway, *The Book of Color Photography* [New York: Alfred A. Knopf, 1979], 18.)

10. "Coloring Photographs," *Photo-Miniature* 4, no. 44 (November, 1902): 357.

11. Telephone conversation between Howard Fast and the author, April 9, 1984.

Detouring the Indian

1. Quoted in Weigle and Fiore, *Santa Fe and Taos*, 17.

2. D. H. Lawrence, "New Mexico," in *Phoenix I*, 147. "New Mexico" was first published in *Survey Graphic* in 1929 (see Weigle and Fiore, 19). Lawrence was deeply affected by his relatively short stays in Taos, New Mexico (1922–23 and 1924–25). He has written powerfully about the impact of the Indian and the land upon an Englishman.

3. Quoted in D. H. Thomas, *The Southwestern Indian Detours* (Phoenix: Hunter Publishing Company, 1978), 46.

4. Ibid., 47.

5. Ibid., 52.

6. Quoted in Albert D. Manchester, "Couriers, Dudes, and Touring Cars," *New Mexico Magazine* (June, 1982): 46.

7. Ibid., 46.

8. Thomas, *The Southwestern Indian Detours*, 297–302.

9. Manchester, "Couriers, Dudes, and Touring Cars," 41.

10. Quoted in Thomas, *The Southwestern Indian Detours*, 48.

11. Thomas, ibid., 252.

12. Quoted in ibid., 196.

13. Ibid., 196.

14. Quoted in ibid., 201–2.

15. Ibid., 249.

16. Harry C. James, *Pages From Hopi History* (Tucson: University of Arizona Press, 1974), 182.

17. Of his "Indian Detour," Sloan continued, "Busses take the tourists out to view the Indian Dances, which are religious ceremonials and naturally not understood as such by the visiting crowds." Quoted in Peter Morse, *John Sloan's Prints: A Catalog Raisonné of the Etchings, Lithographs and Posters* (New Haven: Yale University Press, 1969), 255–56. John Sloan arrived in Santa Fe in 1919 and shortly thereafter became a major presence in the thriving artists' and writers' colony. He spent every summer there, except for one, until 1950. He became a champion of contemporary Indian painting and started, with other Santa Fe associates, the first major national exposition of Indian tribal arts. His own paintings and etchings emphasized the cultural diversity of New Mexico—Indian festivals and ceremonials, Spanish women, and the awesome landscape.

18. Edward T. Hall, *The Silent Language* (New York: Doubleday, 1959; Anchor Books, 1973), 31.

19. Mary McCarthy, *Birds of America* (New York: Harcourt Brace Jovanovich, 1965), 281.

20. Cited in Thomas, *The Southwestern Indian Detours*, 281.

ROUGHING IT IN STYLE

1. Quoted in Turner and Ash, *The Golden Hordes*, 28.

2. Stéphane Mallarmé, *Selected Poetry and Prose*, ed. Mary Ann Caws, trans. Mary Ann and Peter Caws (New York: New Directions, 1982), 16–17. Reprinted by permission of the translators. (Originally published in *Le Parnasse Contemporain*, 1864.)

3. "Gertrude Stein Adores U. S. but Not California!" *New York Herald Tribune*, April 30, 1935. These remarks were prompted when Stein was asked, in an interview, how she felt about returning to San Francisco after nearly forty years.

4. Cited in George Young, *Tourism: Blessing or Blight?* (Harmondsworth, England: Penguin Books, 1973), 39.

4a. Thoreau, "Walking," 176–77.

5. Archibald MacLeish, *America Was Promises* (New York: Duell, Sloan and Pearce, 1939).

6. Santa Fe ad, *Camera Craft* 10 and 11 (1905).

7. Quoted in Earl Pomeroy, *In Search of the Golden West: The Tourist in Western America* (New York: Alfred A. Knopf, 1957), 62.

8. Quoted in Gary Paul Nabhan, *The Desert Smells Like Rain* (San Francisco: North Point Press, 1982), 27. This quote is part of a conversation between a young city boy and Marquita, a Papago woman. Marquita was patiently explaining the human vulnerability of saguaros to the young boy, who had asked whether, lacking a harvesting pole, he could collect fruit from the tall cacti by throwing rocks at the tops to knock the fruit down.

9. Pomeroy, *In Search of the Golden West*, 39.

10. Quoted in Thomas, *The Southwestern Indian Detours*, 139.

11. Steele, *Going Abroad Overland*, 31.

12. Erna Fergusson, "Crusade from Santa Fe," in *North American Review* 242 (1936): 377–78.

13. Edward P. Dozier, *The Pueblo Indians of North America* (New York: Holt, Rinehart and Winston, 1972), 52.

14. Quoted in *Bandelier National Monument* (Santa Fe: School of American Research, 1980), 20, from Adolph F. Bandelier, *Southwestern Journals*, 1880–82.

15. The picture evokes a haunting melancholy of vulgarity, directly attributable to the increasing acquisitiveness of tourist traffic, which was rooted early in this century. It summons the words of H. L. Mencken "that no one ever lost a dime by underestimating the bad taste of the American public."

16. Thomas Merton, *The Collected Poems of Thomas Merton* (New York: New Directions, 1946), 2.

17. Pomeroy, *In Search of the Golden West*, frontispiece. The ecology of the canyon is a diverse one, owing largely to its physical extremes and, therefore, broad and differing climatic zones, which range from desert to sub-Alpine forest. The canyon is two hundred and seventy-seven miles long, an average of ten miles wide, and about one mile deep. It is the world's deepest chasm. In this picture, we have the coniferous forest vegetation of the ponderosa pine and the piñon, distinguishing features of Grand View, a popular tourist stop on the south rim. Woodlands of juniper, a rare bobcat, mule deer, and coyotes are characteristic of the region.

18. Quoted in *The Sacred Path*, ed. John Bierhorst (New York: William Morrow, 1983), 65. Writes Bierhorst: "The native informant, Madeleine Charley, explained that this song 'expresses a joy of living.' "

19. Quoted in Pomeroy, *In Search of the Golden West*, 203.

20. Quoted in *Captain John Hance of the Grand Canyon of Arizona* (published and distributed by the Santa Fe Railway by arrangement with the University of Arizona).

21. Quoted in Pomeroy, *In Search of the Golden West*, frontispiece.

22. Charles H. Coe, *Juggling a Rope* (Pendleton, Oregon: Hamley and Company, 1927), 77–80.

23. For a vivid account of the life of the pioneering Mary Jane Colter, see Virginia L. Grattan's *Mary Colter: Builder Upon the Red Earth* (Flagstaff, Arizona: Northland Press, 1980). Colter, a schoolteacher from St. Paul, Minnesota, became an architect, designer, and decorator for the Fred Harvey Company in 1902. Her major buildings at Grand Canyon include Phantom Ranch, Hermit's Rest, Lookout Studio, Bright Angel Lodge, Hopi House, and the Watchtower. Mary Jane "knew Indian things and had imagination," according to Harvey. All of her architecture—re-creations of another time—had roots in the history of the land.

24. John Wesley Powell, *The Exploration of the Colorado River* (Chicago: University of Chicago Press, 1957), 95. (Originally published in 1875.)

25. Quoted in Peter Hassrick, *The Way West* (New York: Harry N. Abrams, 1984), 136.

26. D. H. Lawrence, "Beyond the Rockies," in *Laughing Horse*, no. 13 (Santa Fe, April, 1926): 10.

27. Quoted in Pomeroy, *In Search of the Golden West*, 37.

28. Quoted in Coke, *Taos and Santa Fe*, 23.

29. Quoted in James Marshall, *Santa Fe: The Railroad That*

Built an Empire (New York: Random House, 1945), 193–94.

30. Willa Cather, *The Song of the Lark* (Boston: Houghton Mifflin, 1943), 102.

31. Berger, *And Our Faces, My Heart, Brief As Photos*, 76–77.

32. Quoted in Huth, *Nature and the American*, 149.

33. Ibid., 150.

34. Herman Melville, *Typee* (London: Constable, 1922), 65. (Originally published in 1846.)

35. Western traveler, quoted in Pomeroy, *In Search of the Golden West*, 34.

36. Ibid., 33–34.

37. Quoted in J. G. Pangborn, *The New Rocky Mountain Tourist* (Chicago: Knight and Leonard, 1878), 3.

38. Quoted in Pomeroy, *In Search of the Golden West*, 36.

39. Quoted in Huth, *Nature and the American*, 151.

40. Ibid., 151.

41. Ibid., 156.

42. It was not until 1890, and then largely owing to the efforts of naturalist and writer John Muir, that the entire Yosemite region around the relatively small state-managed park in Yosemite Valley was made into a national park when a special bill was authorized by President Benjamin Harrison and passed by the Congress in October, 1890, creating a "forest reservation" of more than a million acres.

43. Quoted in Pomeroy, *In Search of the Golden West*, frontispiece.

44. Ibid.

45. Ibid.

46. Sontag, *On Photography*, 99.

47. Quoted in Sontag, *On Photography*, 90.

48. Quoted in Huth, *Nature and the American*, 103.

49. Ibid., 179, 197.

50. Ibid., 151.

THE HOPI

1. Quoted in Edmund Carpenter, *Oh, What a Blow That Phantom Gave Me* (New York: Holt, Rinehart and Winston, 1972), 88. Dr. Carpenter's inquiry into the meaning of "life-lines" in Hopi designs led to this epigraph's illuminating explanation by an elderly Hopi artist from the village of Oraibi.

   "Life-line is the term used to describe a picture of an animal with a line drawn from its mouth to its lungs or heart," writes Carpenter. It is a motif found woven into Pueblo basketry and painted on pots. It is also a motif that is used heavily by the Cree Indians.

1a. Hopi Palatkwapi story, quoted in Harold Courlander, *The Fourth World of the Hopis* (New York: Crown Publishers, 1971; Greenwich, Conn.: Fawcett Publications, 1972), 3.

2. James, *Pages from Hopi History*, 17.

3. Don Talayesva, *Sun Chief*, ed. Leo W. Simmons (New Haven and London: Yale University Press, 1942), xiii.

4. Alexander Alland, Jr., *When the Spider Danced* (New York: Doubleday, Anchor Books, 1975), viii.

5. Quoted in Elsie Clews Parsons, *Pueblo Indian Journal, 1920–21*, American Anthropological Association, Memoirs, no. 32 (Menasha, Wisconsin: The Collegiate Press, George Banta Publishing Company, 1925), 10.

6. Quoted in Dozier, *The Pueblo Indians of North America*, 104.

7. Victor Mindeleff, *A Study of Pueblo Architecture, Tusayan and Cibola* (Washington, D.C.: Bureau of American Ethnology, 8th annual report, 1891), 140.

8. Ibid., 142.

9. Don Talayesva, *Sun Chief*, 51.

10. Thomas, *The Southwestern Indian Detours*, 198. Quoted by permission.

11. Quoted in McLuhan, *Touch the Earth*, 39.

12. See Wayne Dennis, *The Hopi Child* (New York and London: D. Appleton-Century, 1940), 31, and Laura Thompson and Alice Joseph, *The Hopi Way* (Chicago: University of Chicago Press, 1944), 50.

13. Walter Hough, *The Hopi Indians* (Cedar Rapids, Iowa: The Torch Press, 1915), 82.

14. Quoted in Parsons, *A Pueblo Indian Journal*, 31.

15. Quoted in Grattan, *Mary Colter*, 19.

16. Edward S. Curtis, *The North American Indian*, ed. Frederick Webb Hodge, 20 vols. (written, illustrated and published by Edward S. Curtis), 12: 21.

17. Ibid., 43.

18. Quoted in Edmund Carpenter, *Eskimo Realities* (New York: Holt, Rinehart and Winston, 1973), 193.

19. Ruth Bunzel, *The Pueblo Potter: A Study of Creative Imagination in Primitive Art* (New York: Columbia University Press, 1929; Dover Publications, 1972), 8, 29.

20. Jesse Walter Fewkes, *Archeological Expedition to Arizona in 1895* (Washington, D.C.: Seventeenth Annual Report

of the Bureau of American Ethnology to the Secretary of the Smithsonian Institution, 1895–96), pt. II, 661.

21. Ibid.
22. Don Talayesva, *Sun Chief*, 220.
23. Quoted in Gertrude Prokosch Kurath and Antonio Garcia, *Music and Dance of the Tewa Pueblos* (Santa Fe: Museum of New Mexico Press, 1969), 169.
24. Don Talayesva, *Sun Chief*, 42.
25. Emory Sekaquaptewa, "Hopi Indian Ceremonies," in *Seeing with a Native Eye*, ed. Walter Holden Capps (New York: Harper and Row, 1976), 39.
26. Don Talayesva, *Sun Chief*, 21–22.
27. Ibid., 21.
28. Harold S. Colton, *Hopi Kachina Dolls* (Albuquerque: University of New Mexico Press, 1949), 44, 50, 76.
29. Vincent Scully, *Pueblo: Mountain, Village, Dance* (New York: The Viking Press, 1975), 270.
30. Hough, *The Hopi Indians*, 78.
31. Quoted in A. R. Radcliffe-Brown, *Structure and Function in Primitive Society* (Glencoe, Illinois: The Free Press, 1952), 159.
32. Cited in Webb and Weinstein, *Dwellers at the Source*, 85.
33. Theodore Roosevelt, "The Hopi Snake Dance," in *The Outlook*, October 18, 1913, 365.
34. Hough, *The Hopi Indians*, 219.
35. John L. Stoddard, *John Lawson Stoddard's Lectures*, 10 vols. (Boston: Balch Brothers, 1918), 10: 148, 153.
36. Santa Fe Advertising, Santa Fe Transportation Company, bulletin no. 21, April 25, 1929.
37. D. H. Lawrence, *The Plumed Serpent* (London: William Heinemann, 1926), 125.
38. D. H. Lawrence, "New Mexico," in *Phoenix I*, 141.
39. Hough, *The Hopi Indians*, 223–24.
40. Quoted in Alexander M. Stephen, *Hopi Journal*, ed. Elsie Clews Parsons (New York: Columbia University Press, 1936; AMS Press, 1969), pt. 1, 679. They are addressed, and then an invocation is made. Feathers are among the most important objects employed in Pueblo ceremonies. Feathers of the turkey, for example, are potent in inducing rain. Those of the eagle or the hawk pertain especially to the power of the sun; a breast feather of an eagle is chosen as an individual prayer-bearer. The feathers of an owl, like the owl itself, are generally regarded as having similar influence; but sometimes the feather of this bird is beneficial, it is believed, in making peach trees yield abundantly. (Jesse Walter Fewkes, *Designs on Prehistoric Hopi Pottery* [Washington, D.C.: Thirty-third Annual Report, Bureau of American Ethnology, 1911–12].)
41. Theodore Roosevelt, "The Hopi Snake Dance," 370.
42. "The term 'totemism' is used for a form of social organization and magico-religious practice, of which the central feature is the association of certain groups (usually clans or lineages) within a tribe with certain classes of animate or inanimate things, the several groups being associated with distinct classes." (From *Notes and Queries on Anthropology*, a collective work published by the Royal Anthropological Institute, London, 6th ed., 1951, 192.)
43. Quoted in Doug Boyd, *Rolling Thunder* (New York: Dell Publishing Company, 1974), 98.
44. Mischa Titiev, *Old Oraibi*, Papers of the Peabody Museum of American Archaeology and Ethnology, Harvard University, vol. 22, no. 1 (Cambridge, Mass.: Peabody Museum, 1944), 151.
45. Don Talayevsa, *Sun Chief*, 42.
46. H. R. Voth, *The Oraibi Summer Snake Ceremony*, Anthropological Series, vol. 3, no. 4 (Chicago: Field Columbian Museum, publication no. 83, November, 1903), 340.
47. Theodore Roosevelt, "The Hopi Snake Dance," 371. Speculation runs high as to how the Snake priests can handle the rattlesnakes in such manner with impunity. There is no *real* explanation for the immunity of the dancers. Conjecture ranges wild: It has been said that the snakes are defanged prior to the ceremony; it has also been asserted that their indifference is due to a "medicine" they are given, the inference being that they are drugged. All these theories are unfounded. The matter or mystery is not easily explained. Voth has suggested that an explanation may be found in "the careful handling of the snakes" not so much in the "*frequency* of handling, but rather in the *manner* of handling." And Roosevelt proposed that "the snake priests either naturally possess or develop the same calm power over these serpents that certain men have over bees"; but at the same time he could not understand "why the rattlers were not all maddened by the treatment they received in the kiva, and

again when thrown [so wildly] at the base of Snake Altar Rock at the end of the ceremony."

48. Voth, *The Oraibi Summer Snake Ceremony*, 340.

49. Jesse Walter Fewkes, *Tusayan Flute and Snake Ceremonies* (Washington, D.C.: Nineteenth Annual Report of the Bureau of American Ethnology, 1901).

50. Quoted in *The Potlatch: A Strict Law Bids Us Dance*, a sixty-minute documentary by filmmaker Dennis Wheeler, 1976.

51. Quoted in Joseph Epes Brown, *The Spiritual Legacy of the North American Indian* (New York: The Crossroad Publishing Company, 1982), 123.

52. Norman Mailer, *The Armies of the Night* (New York: The New American Library, 1968; Signet Books, 1968), 319.

53. Kevin Brownlow, *The War, the West and the Wilderness* (New York: Alfred A. Knopf, 1979), 443.

54. Curtis, *The North American Indian*, 155. Edward S. Curtis, ethnographer, photographer and filmmaker, made many visits to the Hopi pueblos. He first witnessed the Snake Dance in the year 1900 at the pueblo of Walpi. Subsequent trips were made over the next twelve years. In the year 1912 he was initiated into the Snake ceremony. His portraiture of Hopi life is outstanding and affords a rare glimpse into the intricacies of Pueblo culture.

55. Webb and Weinstein, *Dwellers at the Source*, 88.

56. Voth, *The Oraibi Summer Snake Ceremony*, 346. H. R. Voth, missionary, observer, and ethnologist, took notes and pictures, and made sketches of the Snake ceremony at Oraibi on three separate occasions during the month of August in the years 1896, 1898, and 1900.

57. Webb and Weinstein, *Dwellers at the Source*, 88.

58. Both Roosevelt and Voth commented on the rough handling of the snakes and wondered why it did not anger the reptiles and cause them to strike out. Bites were rare, however, and were usually attributed to a man being impure of heart and unworthy of participation in the ceremony. In his autobiography, Sun Chief, a Hopi, explains this point further. As a young man, he tells us, he saw a man who "was bitten by a snake in one of the dances and [who] nearly lost his life. He must have had a very bad heart." Sun Chief was raised to believe that "when the dancers are not pure or do not pay attention to their business, the snakes get angry. [Furthermore], if a dancer has slept with a woman during the ceremony he will become sick or unable to perform, or the snake may bite him in the dance." Remembering another incident, he added, "Once a leader was bitten while hunting for snakes; and the old people tell of men who have died of snakebites when they have failed to do their duty."

59. Webb and Weinstein, *Dwellers at the Source*, 89.

THE NAVAJO

1. Quoted in Kenneth Brower, ed., *Navajo Wildlands* (New York: Ballantine Books, 1967), 16.

1a. Old Mexican, Navaho, quoted in Walter Dyk, *A Navajo Autobiography* (New York: The Viking Fund, Inc., Publications in Anthropology, no. 8, 1947), 164.

2. Willa Cather, *Death Comes for the Archbishop* (New York: Alfred A. Knopf, 1927; reprint, 1967), 53.

3. Quoted in Richard Hobson, *Navaho Acquisitive Values*, Papers of the Peabody Museum of American Archaeology and Ethnology, Harvard University, vol. 42, no. 3 (Cambridge, Mass.: Peabody Museum, 1954), 25.

4. Ibid., 21.

5. Ibid., 20.

6. Ibid., 26.

7. Cited in Clyde Kluckhohn and Dorothea Leighton, *The Navaho* (Cambridge, Mass.: Harvard University Press, 1946; New York: Anchor Books and the American Museum of Natural History, 1962), 90.

8. Tony Berlant and Mary Kahlenberg, *Art in America*, July–August, 1972, 78.

9. Quoted in Kluckhohn and Leighton, *The Navaho*, 70.

10. Cited in McLuhan, *Touch the Earth*, 176.

11. N. Scott Momaday, *The Names* (New York: Harper and Row, 1976), 119–20.

THE RIO GRANDE AND WESTERN PUEBLOS

1. Quoted in Gibson, *The Santa Fe and Taos Colonies*, 220.

1a. Harriet Monroe, quoted in Weigle and Fiore, *Santa Fe and Taos*, 17.

2. Dozier, *The Pueblo Indians of North America*, 3.

3. Quoted in Weigle and Fiore, *Santa Fe and Taos*, 14.

4. Cather, *Death Comes for the Archbishop*, 95.

5. Charles F. Lummis, *Mesa, Cañon, and Pueblo* (New York and London: The Century Company, 1925), 426.

6. Lawrence, "Taos," in *Phoenix I*, 101–2.

7. Alland, *When the Spider Danced*, 181.

8. Quoted in June Du Bois, *W. R. Leigh* (Kansas City: The Lowell Press, 1977), 55–56. When the young ethnologist Frank Hamilton Cushing visited Zuni for the first time in 1879 he wrote with a similar awe and excitement of his arrival at the pueblo: "Below and beyond me was suddenly revealed a great red and yellow sand-plain. It merged into long stretches of gray, indistinct hill-lands in the western distance, distorted by mirages and sand-clouds, and overshadowed towards the north by two grand solitary buttes of rock. . . . Imagine numberless long, box-shaped, adobe ranches connected with one another in extended rows and squares, with others, less and less numerous, piled up on them lengthwise and crosswise, in two, three, even six stories, each receding from the one below it like the steps of a broken stairflight—as it were a gigantic pyramidal mud honeycomb with far outstretching base,—and you can gain a fair conception of the architecture of Zuni." Frank Hamilton Cushing, *Zuni: Selected Writings of Frank Hamilton Cushing*, ed. Jesse Green (Lincoln: University of Nebraska Press, 1979), 47–48.

9. Quoted in Brown, *The Spiritual Legacy of the North American Indian*, 120.

10. Mindeleff, *A Study of Pueblo Architecture, Tusayan and Cibola*, 101–2.

11. Talayesva, *Sun Chief*, 58.

12. Quoted in Webb and Weinstein, *Dwellers at the Source*, 144.

13. Hough, *The Hopi Indians*, 62, 66.

14. Quoted in John Adair, *The Navaho and Pueblo Silversmiths* (Norman: University of Oklahoma Press, 1944), 122.

15. Virginia More Roediger, *Ceremonial Costumes of the Pueblo Indians* (Berkeley and Los Angeles: University of California Press, 1961), 141. ". . . turquoise, jet and coral require much drilling," continues Roediger. "When a number of rough beads have been drilled they are strung in a tight column on a length of cord and the whole string is ground to an even size on a slab of sandstone [as seen in the picture] or between two stones." Turquoise is a highly prized gem and has important historical, economic, and religious significance within Pueblo culture. At Zuni, for example, "after the sale of wool in the spring a man liquidates his debts and invests the balance in turquoise," wrote anthropologist Ruth Bunzel in 1932. In addition, "the amount of turquoise worn by an impersonator," continued Bunzel, "is limited only by his borrowing capacity. The necklaces cover the whole chest, frequently also the whole back. . . . The way of wearing the necklaces is indicative of rank and position. Necklaces front and back indicate a Katcina of importance; necklaces doubled over and worn close to the throat are a badge of society membership." (Ruth Bunzel, *Zuni Katcinas* [Washington, D.C.: Forty-seventh Annual Report of the Bureau of American Ethnology, 1932], 871. Cited in Roediger.)

16. Quoted in John Fire Lame Deer and Richard Erdoes, *Lame Deer, Seeker of Visions* (New York: Simon and Schuster, 1972), 155–59.

17. Mircea Eliade, *Shamanism: Archaic Techniques of Ecstasy* (Princeton, N.J.: Princeton University Press, Bollingen Series 76, 1972), 510. (Originally published in French as *Le Chamanisme et les techniques archaïques de l'extase* [Paris: Librairie Payot], 1951.)

18. Roediger, *Ceremonial Costumes of the Pueblo Indians*, 193.

19. Ibid., 184.

20. Momaday, *The Names*, 135.

21. Ibid., 128–29.

22. See Curtis, *The North American Indian*, vol. 17 (1926): 145–46.

23. Quoted in Watson Smith, *Kiva Decorations at Awatovi and Kawaika-a*, Papers of the Peabody Museum of Archaeology and Ethnology, Harvard University, vol. 37 (Cambridge, Mass.: Peabody Museum, 1952), 225.

24. John Collier, *Patterns and Ceremonials of the Indians of the Southwest* (New York: E. P. Dutton, 1949), 63.

25. Scully, *Pueblo: Mountain, Village, Dance*, 187.

26. Quoted in Smith, *Kiva Decorations at Awatovi and Kawaika-a*, 225.

27. Ibid.

28. Norman Quyintewa in *The Shadow Catcher*, a feature docudrama, produced, directed, and written by T. C. McLuhan, 1975.

29. Cited in Weigle and Fiore, *Santa Fe and Taos*, 17.

30. Francis La Flesche, *The Osage Tribe: Rite of the Wa Xo-Be* (Washington, D.C.: Bureau of American Ethnology, 1928).

SELECTED BIBLIOGRAPHY

ADAIR, JOHN. *The Navaho and Pueblo Silversmiths.* Norman: University of Oklahoma Press, 1944.

BARTHES, ROLAND. *The Eiffel Tower and Other Mythologies.* New York: Hill and Wang, 1979.

BARTLETT, SIR FREDERIC C. *Remembering.* Cambridge, England: Cambridge University Press, 1932.

BENEDICT, RUTH. *Patterns of Culture.* Boston: Houghton Mifflin, 1934.

BROWN, JOSEPH EPES. *The Spiritual Legacy of the North American Indian.* New York: The Crossroad Publishing Company, 1982.

BRYANT, JR., KEITH L. *History of the Atchison, Topeka and Santa Fe Railway.* New York: Macmillan, 1974.

BUNZEL, RUTH. *The Pueblo Potter: A Study of Creative Imagination in Primitive Art.* New York: Columbia University Press, 1929.

CAPPS, WALTER HOLDEN. *Seeing with a Native Eye.* New York: Harper and Row, 1976.

CATHER, WILLA. *Death Comes for the Archbishop.* New York: Alfred A. Knopf, 1927.

_____. *Song of the Lark.* Boston: Houghton Mifflin, 1943.

CHONA, MARIA. *Autobiography of a Papago Woman.* Edited by Ruth Underhill. Menasha, Wisconsin: The American Anthropological Association, Memoirs, vol. 46, 1936.

COE, BRIAN. *The History of Movie Photography.* Westfield, N. J.: Eastview Editions, 1981.

COKE, VAN DEREN. *Taos and Santa Fe: The Artist's Environment, 1882–1942.* Albuquerque: University of New Mexico Press for the Amon Carter Museum of Western Art, 1963.

COURLANDER, HAROLD. *The Fourth World of the Hopi.* New York: Crown Publishers, 1971.

CURTIS, NATALIE. *The Indians' Book: Songs and Legends of the American Indians.* New York: Dover Publications, 1968. (Originally published in 1907.)

CUSHING, FRANK H. *My Adventures in Zuni.* Palo Alto, California: American West Publishing Company, 1905.

DENNIS, WAYNE. *The Hopi Child.* New York and London: D. Appleton-Century, 1940.

DYK, WALTER, recorder. *Son of Old Man Hat: A Navaho Autobiography.* New York: Harcourt, Brace, 1938.

_____. *A Navaho Autobiography.* New York: Viking Fund Publications in Anthropology, no. 8, 1947.

EMERSON, RALPH WALDO. *The Journals and Miscellaneous Notebooks.* Edited by Alfred R. Ferguson et al. 14 vols. Cambridge, Mass.: Harvard University, the Belknap Press, 1960–78.

FERGUSSON, ERNA. "Crusade from Santa Fe." *North American Review* 242 (1936).

FEWKES, JESSE WALTER. *Tusayan Flute and Snake Ceremonies.* Washington, D.C.: Nineteenth Annual Report, Bureau of American Ethnology, 1901.

GIBSON, ARRELL MORGAN. *The Santa Fe and Taos Colonies: Age of the Muses, 1900–1942.* Norman: University of Oklahoma Press, 1938.

HALL, EDWARD T. *The Silent Language.* New York: Doubleday, 1959.

HILL, W. W. *The Agricultural and Hunting Methods of the Navaho Indians.* New Haven: Yale University Press, 1938.

HUTH, HANS. *Nature and the American: Three Centuries of Changing Attitudes.* Berkeley and Los Angeles: University of California Press, 1957; Lincoln: University of Nebraska Press, 1972.

JAMES, HARRY C. *Pages from Hopi History.* Tucson: University of Arizona Press, 1974.

KLUCKHOHN, CLYDE, and DOROTHEA LEIGHTON. *The Navaho.* Cambridge, Mass.: Harvard University Press, 1946.

KURATH, GERTRUDE PROKOSCH, with ANTONIO GARCIA. *Music and Dance of the Tewa Pueblos.* Santa Fe: Museum of New Mexico Press, 1969.

LAWRENCE, D. H. *Phoenix I: The Posthumous Papers of D. H. Lawrence.* Edited with an introduction by Edward D. McDonald. London: William Heinemann, 1936; New York: The Viking Press, 1939.

LEE, DOROTHY. *Freedom and Culture.* Englewood Cliffs, N.J.: Prentice-Hall, 1959.

LUMMIS, CHARLES F. *Mesa, Cañon and Pueblo.* New York and London: The Century Company, 1925.

MACCANNELL, DEAN. *The Tourist.* New York: Schocken Books, 1976.

MacLeish, Archibald. *Collected Poems, 1917–1952*. Boston: Houghton Mifflin, 1952.

McLuhan, T. C. *Touch the Earth: A Self-Portrait of Indian Existence*. New York: Outerbridge and Dienstfrey, 1971; Simon and Schuster, A Touchstone Book, 1972.

————, and A. D. Coleman. *Portraits from North American Indian Life by Edward S. Curtis*. New York: Outerbridge and Lazard and the American Museum of Natural History, 1972.

Marshall, James. *Santa Fe: The Railroad That Built an Empire*. New York: Random House, 1945.

Marx, Leo. *The Machine in the Garden*. New York: Oxford University Press, 1964.

Miller, Perry. *Errand into the Wilderness*. New York: Harper and Row, 1964.

————. *Nature's Nation*. Cambridge, Mass.: Harvard University, the Belknap Press, 1967.

Momaday, N. Scott. *The Names*. New York: Harper and Row, Colophon Books, 1976.

————. *The Way to Rainy Mountain*. Albuquerque: University of New Mexico Press, 1969.

Nabhan, Gary Paul. *The Desert Smells Like Rain: A Naturalist in Papago Country*. San Francisco: North Point Press, 1982.

Nash, Roderick. *Wilderness and the American Mind*. New Haven: Yale University Press, 1967.

Novak, Barbara. *Nature and Culture: American Landscape and Painting, 1825–1875*. New York: Oxford University Press, 1980.

Ortiz, Alfonso, ed. *New Perspectives on the Pueblos*. Albuquerque: University of New Mexico Press, 1972.

————. *The Tewa World: Space, Being, and Becoming in a Pueblo Society*. Chicago: University of Chicago Press, 1969.

Parsons, Elsie Clews. *A Pueblo Indian Journal, 1920–21*. American Anthropological Association, Memoirs, no. 32. Menasha, Wisconsin: The Collegiate Press, George Banta Publishing Company, 1925.

Pinchot, Gifford. *Breaking New Ground*. New York: Harcourt, Brace, 1947.

Pomeroy, Earl. *In Search of the Golden West: The Tourist in Western America*. New York: Alfred A. Knopf, 1957.

Quigley, Jr., Martin. *Magic Shadows: The Story of the Origin of Motion Pictures*. New York: Quigley Publishing Company, 1960.

Radcliffe-Brown, A. R. *Structure and Function in Primitive Society*. Glencoe, Illinois: The Free Press, 1952.

Reeve, Kay Aiken. *The Making of an American Place: The Development of Santa Fe and Taos, New Mexico, as an American Cultural Center, 1898–1942*. College Station, Texas: Ph.D. diss., Texas A & M University, 1977.

Reichard, Gladys A. *Social Life of the Navajo Indians*. New York: Columbia University Press, 1928.

Russell, Bertrand. *The Impact of Science on Society*. London: Allen and Unwin, 1952.

Scully, Vincent. *Pueblo: Mountain, Village, Dance*. New York: The Viking Press, 1975.

Smith, Henry Nash. *Virgin Land: The American West as Symbol and Myth*. Cambridge, Mass.: Harvard University Press, 1950.

Sontag, Susan. *On Photography*. New York: Dell Publishing Company, 1973.

Steele, David M. *Going Abroad Overland: Studies of Places and People in the Far West*. New York and London: G.P. Putnam's Sons, The Knickerbocker Press, 1917.

Stilgoe, John R. *Metropolitan Corridor: Railroads and the American Scene*. New Haven and London: Yale University Press, 1983.

Taft, Robert. *Artists and Illustrators of the Old West, 1850–1900*. New York: Charles Scribner's Sons, 1953.

Talayesva, Don. *Sun Chief*. Edited by Leo W. Simmons. New Haven and London: Yale University Press, 1942.

Thomas, D. H. *The Southwestern Indian Detours*. Phoenix: Hunter Publishing Company, 1978.

Thompson, Laura, and Alice Joseph. *The Hopi Way*. Chicago: University of Chicago Press, 1944.

Thoreau, Henry David. *Excursions*. New York: Corinth Books, 1962. (Originally published in 1863.)

Titiev, Mischa. *Old Oraibi: A Study of the Hopi Indians of the Third Mesa*. Papers of the Peabody Museum of American Archaeology and Ethnology, Harvard University, vol. 22, no. 1. Cambridge, Mass.: Peabody Museum, 1944.

Turner, Louis, and John Ash. *The Golden Hordes: International Tourism and the Pleasure Periphery*. London: Constable, 1975.

UDALL, STEWART L. *The Quiet Crisis*. New York: Holt, Rinehart and Winston, 1963.

VOTH, H. R. *The Oraibi Summer Snake Ceremony*. Anthropological Series, vol. III, no. 4. Chicago: Field Columbian Museum, Publication no. 83, November, 1903.

WATERS, FRANK. *The Book of the Hopi*. New York: The Viking Press, 1963.

WATERS, L. L. *Steel Rails to Santa Fe*. Lawrence: University of Kansas Press, 1950.

WEIGLE, MARTA, and KYLE FIORE. *Santa Fe and Taos: The Writer's Era, 1916–1941*. Santa Fe: Ancient City Press, 1982.

WYMAN, WALKER D., and CLIFTON B. KROEBER, eds. *The Frontier in Perspective*. Madison: University of Wisconsin Press, 1957.

YOUNG, GEORGE. *Tourism: Blessing or Blight?* Harmondsworth, England: Penguin Books, 1976.

PICTURE CREDITS

THE KOPPLIN COLLECTION
PHOTOGRAPHERS

Fay Cooper Cole: page 89. Aaron B. Craycraft: page 55. Fred Harvey: page 186. Fred Harvey and Company: page 63. W. H. Jackson: page 100 *top*. W. H. Jackson & Co.: pages 91, 112, 163. Edward H. Kemp: pages 49, 52, 59, 66 *top*, 81, 125. William E. Kopplin: pages 60, 76, 90, 115, 120, 143, 146, 165, 167, 168, 185, 188, 191. Moore, Hubbell & Co.: page 64. Jesse L. Nausbaum: pages 161, 181. The Santa Fe Railway: pages 51, 61, 65, 66 *bottom*, 68, 85, 93 *top*, 97, 101, 111, 122, 129, 147, 151, 154, 155, 171, 174 *bottom*, 177, 189. William H. Simpson: pages 93 *bottom*, 100 *bottom*, 102, 110. A. C. Vromans: page 118. Photographer unknown: pages 56, 69, 71, 72, 73, 75, 77, 78 *top*, 78 *bottom*, 79, 80, 82, 83, 84 *top*, 84 *bottom*, 92, 94, 95, 98, 99, 103, 105, 106, 107 *top*, 107 *bottom*, 108, 109, 114, 121, 124, 127, 128, 148, 149, 150, 152, 153, 159, 160, 164, 169, 172, 173, 174, 175, 176, 179, 180, 182, 183, 184 *top*, 184 *bottom*, 190.

SOURCES OF ILLUSTRATIONS

Courtesy of American Museum of Natural History, Department of Library Services, New York City: page 14 (neg. 42013, photograph by C. Mayer)

Courtesy of Colorado Historical Society, Denver, Colorado: page 6 (neg. 08763), page 35 (neg. J-30,037)

Denver Public Library, Western History Division: page 8, photograph by Horace S. Poley

Courtesy of Kraushaar Galleries, New York City: pages 44, 45

La Fonda Hotel, Santa Fe, New Mexico: page 17

Library of Congress, Washington, D.C.: page 12 (neg. 30414 USZ62737), page 18 (neg. 11068), original map redrawn by Christopher L. Brest

Courtesy of Museum of New Mexico, Santa Fe, New Mexico: page 2 (neg. 38211, photograph by J. R. Riddle), page 3 (neg. 47181, photograph by Keystone Photo Service), page 9 (neg. 46939), page 39 (neg. 38193, photograph by El Tovar Studio)

Courtesy of Santa Fe Collection of Southwestern Art: pages 29, 30, 31, 32

Courtesy of Santa Fe Railway, Public Relations Department, Photography: pages 7, 27, 42

SOURCES OF INDIAN DRAWINGS

Pages 46, 116, 118, 156, 162: Le Roy H. Appleton, *American Indian Design and Decoration*. New York: Dover Publications, Inc., 1971. Pages 86, 113: Harry C. James, *The Hopi Indians*. Caldwell, Idaho: The Caxton Printers, Ltd., 1956. Pages 158, 170: H. P. Mera, *Pueblo Designs*. New York: Dover Publications, Inc., 1970. Pages 54, 96: Maria Naylor, editor, *Authentic Indian Designs*. New York: Dover Publications, Inc., 1975. Page 186: Virginia More Roediger, *Ceremonial Costumes of the Pueblo Indians*. Berkeley and Los Angeles: University of California Press, 1941. Pages 48, 50, 58, 62, 70, 88, 104, 144, 166, 178: Dorothy Smith Sides, *Decorative Art of the Southwestern Indians*. New York: Dover Publications, Inc., 1961. Pages 126, 130: Frank Waters, *The Book of the Hopi*. New York: Penguin Books, 1977.

INDEX

Page numbers in italic refer to
material in Notes and References.